STEP BY

GW00362048

Using Ability
on the Amstrad PC

Using Ability

on the Amstrad PC

Samuel Kennington

Heinemann Professional Publishing

Heinemann Professional Publishing Ltd
Halley Court, Jordan Hill, Oxford OX2 8EJ

OXFORD   LONDON   MELBOURNE   AUCKLAND

First published 1988

British Library Cataloguing in Publication Data
McBride, P.K.
  Using Ability on the Amstrad PC.
  1. Amstrad microcomputer systems. Software
  packages. Ability
  I. Title
  005.36'9

ISBN 0-434-90221-7

Typeset by JCA Typesetting, Ringwood, Hampshire
Printed in England by L R Printing Ltd, Crawley, Sussex.

Contents

Contents

PART ONE

Using Ability

■ SECTION 1
All·you need is Ability

That is not entirely true, but it is near enough to make a good heading. With its word processing, database, spreadsheet, graph-making, communications and presentation software, the Ability package could well provide most or all of the computing needs of some offices and of many individual users. In fact, I wonder how many people will ever use all its facilities to the full.

There is a lot to Ability. Each of its sections has the same kind of range and power that you would find in full-priced individual packages. Now that should mean that it ought to take a long while to learn how to use everything properly, but it does not. One of the key features of Ability is that it is a truly *integrated* suite. Data can be passed freely between different parts of the system – you can use numbers from a spreadsheet to make a graph; bring names and other details from a database into a report that you are writing; in fact, you can take any data from any file and use it in another. This gives the whole system a tremendous power and flexibility, and we will be looking at how to use this as we go on.

But there is another aspect of this integration that is perhaps even more important to the new user. There is a common set of commands that runs right across all parts of the software; and even where specialised commands are needed, they have the same basic feel and method of operation. This means that once you have learnt how to use one part of the system, you are already well on the way to knowing how to use another part. Buy yourself a separate word-processor, database, spreadsheet and communications package, and you will have to start learning from scratch each time!

■ SECTION 1
All you need is Ability

Briefly then, what can you do with Ability?

WRITE

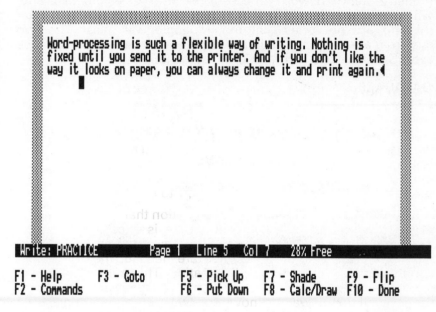

FIGURE 1-1 The Write screen

Write is Ability's word-processor. Use it to write letters, reports, theses, articles, even books – this book is being written using Write, and it is proving to be very efficient as well as convenient. As with all good word-processors, correcting and editing text is quick and easy. Blocks of text – anything from a single word or sentence to whole pages – can be picked up and moved from one part of a document to another. You can set Write off on a search for a particular word or phrase, and it will find it in seconds, even in the longest documents, and having found the text it was looking for, Write can replace this automatically with a new word or phrase. Items that need to be highlighted when the document is printed, can be set in bold or italic typefaces, or underlined, and the size of the page and layout of the text can be easily adjusted. There is a limit to the size of files that the system can handle, but it

11

is in the order of 100k. In practice, you would rarely want to use files that large — 100k is about 14,000 words.

Compared to WordStar, which is generally regarded as the industry standard word-processor, Write is easier to use, and, while it does not have all of WordStar's facilities, the ones that are missing are not ones that many people will miss! The two systems are not compatible, but any software that can use WordStar files can read text produced with Write.

DATABASE

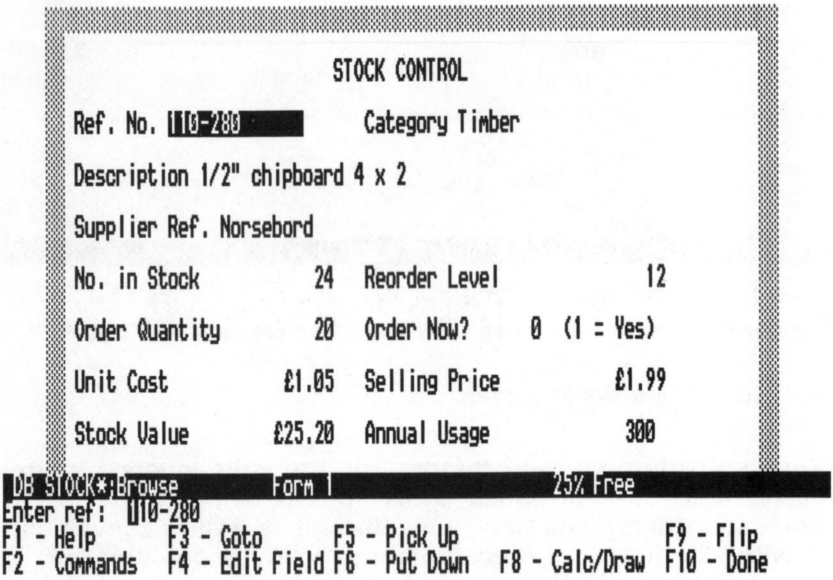

```
                        STOCK CONTROL

   Ref. No. 110-280            Category Timber

   Description 1/2" chipboard 4 x 2

   Supplier Ref. Norsebord

   No. in Stock        24    Reorder Level            12

   Order Quantity      20    Order Now?    0  (1 = Yes)

   Unit Cost        £1.05    Selling Price         £1.99

   Stock Value     £25.20    Annual Usage            300

 DB STOCK* Browse        Form 1                   25% Free
Enter ref: 110-280
F1 - Help       F3 - Goto       F5 - Pick Up                  F9 - Flip
F2 - Commands   F4 - Edit Field F6 - Put Down   F8 - Calc/Draw F10 - Done
```

FIGURE 1-2 The Database screen

■ SECTION 1
All you need is Ability

The Database offers a simple-to-use, but powerful, card-index-style filing system, which can be used to store any kind of organised data. In a business, the most common uses would probably be in stock control or for customer or supplier files. It will hold names, addresses, product information, details of how much is owed, when payment was last made, and so on. And it will do any calculations that are needed within each record. When you want to recall information, the software can hunt through the files and pull out an individual record or all of those that belong to a particular group. It can produce summary reports, and give totals if needed, or can be used for mail-merging. This latter facility, the production of personalised circulars, makes full use of the integration between the Database and Write.

In the past, smaller businesses have tended to be a little slow in starting to use databases. Could that be because they had not discovered the power and simplicity of the Ability system?

All you need is Ability

SPREADSHEET

```
      A              B              C           D       E    F    G
1  What if?
2                 Wage Increase           15%
3                 Price Increase         2.5%
4                 Productivity       <CIRC>      0.01
5  Unit Costs
6  Materials          £40.00        £40.00
7  Labour,etc         £60.00        £69.00
8  Total Unit cost   £100.00       £109.00
9
10 Sell at           £150.00       £153.75
11
12 Units Made     £10,000.00    £10,000.00  ████████
13 Var. Costs  £1,000,000.00 £1,090,000.00
14 Fixed Costs   £300,000.00   £300,000.00
15 Total Costs £1,300,000.00 £1,390,000.00
16
17 Income      £1,500,000.00 £1,537,500.00
18
19 Profit        £200,000.00   £147,500.00
20
Spreadsheet: RISES                         27% Free
LABEL  Enter D12:
F1 - Help       F3 - Goto       F5 - Pick Up   F7 - Shade      F9 - Flip
F2 - Commands   F4 - Edit Field F6 - Put Down  F8 - Calc/Draw  F10 - Done
```

FIGURE 1-3 The Spreadsheet screen

The Spreadsheet is a number-crunching tool. Use it for totalling the accounts, for doing the payroll, job-costing, invoicing, discounted cash flows, forecasting and a hundred and one other routine, and not so routine, calculations. The great beauty of the spreadsheet is that once you have built the basic 'model', and worked out the formulae that link the values, it is there to be re-used again and again. At a simple level, this may be an invoicing spreadsheet, where items are totalled and VAT added in. Once the model has been created, the salesperson need only write the item values on the blank sheet to produce an invoice. A more complex spreadsheet model might explore the profitability of a planned investment. Different costings and different levels of sales can be fed into the sheet, to find the potential return under varying conditions. If the calculations had to be done by hand, it would take long enough to get a result from one set of figures. With a spreadsheet, a whole set of scenarios can be explored in a single, unflustered, working session.

Ability's Spreadsheet does not have the full range of functions that are found in Lotus 1-2-3 or SuperCalc4 (the two leading spreadsheet systems), but – as with Write and WordStar – those things that are missing are not ones that most people use.

GRAPH

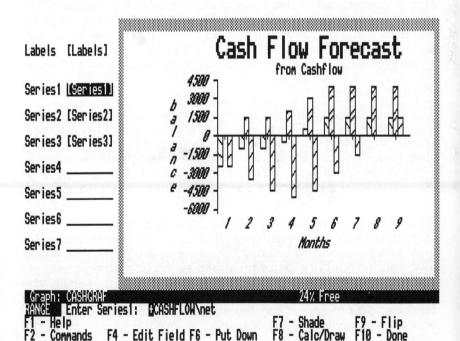

FIGURE 1-4 The Graph screen

The Graph facility is perhaps best used as an adjunct to the spreadsheet. The routines in this section will turn your figures into attractive and meaningful line graphs, bar and pie charts. These will give a better overview of what's going on, than can be had from a solid table of numbers. Used with the word-processor, a graph can do much to enliven a report or enhance a thesis.

COMMUNICATE

The last, but not least, of Ability's sections is Communicate. Add in a modem, and this will enable you to link your PC to other computers, to act as a terminal to a mainframe, or to access that ever-growing host of database and electronic mail facilities that can be found at the other end of a telephone line. Get the latest share information, book train or theatre tickets, swap ideas and software with other enthusiasts, send a letter – instantly – to the other side of the world – it can all be done via Communicate.

PRESENTATION!

Though included within the Ability package, this is not an integral part of the suite. With it you can take snapshots of graphs, spreadsheets and documents and assemble them into a computer slide show, with additional text and even music if you want it! In some situations this can be an effective way of getting a message across to a group of people. Do you ever need to make a presentation at a conference? This could be the way to do it.

If you take each module in isolation, there is no doubt that you can find other software on the market that is just as good or better. But they cost far more. To put together a set of programs that would give you the same range of functions as the one Ability package, you will pay anything from £300 to £1,000+. In any case, the whole is greater than the sum of the parts, and Ability is more than just a word-processor, database, spreadsheet, graph-maker and communications package. It is an *integrated* suite, and the way that the modules can interrelate gives Ability exceptional power and flexibility.

■ SECTION 2
Before you start

If you have not done so already, follow the instructions in the 'What To Do First' leaflet, to copy the Ability files onto your hard disk, or onto a set of floppy disks.

Floppy Disk Systems

Three floppies will be needed here; one should be formatted using the **FORMAT /S** option, and should have COMMAND.COM copied onto it from the MS-DOS system disk. This will become your working copy of the Ability System disk, and can be used to start up the computer from cold. The other two disks can be formatted with the simpler **format** command, which leaves rather more space available for data storage. One of these disks will become the working Ability help disk, and the other will be used for storing data files – the text written with the word-processor, the records held in a database and so on.

Do make sure that you copy the help file (labelled ABILITY.HLP, on the system disk) onto that first data disk. If you do not do this, you will have to swap the disks over every time you want to use the built-in help functions. (It is an irony of the Ability system that the so-called help disk does not have the help file on it!)

Hard Disk Systems

Hard-disk users who will be using Ability to write confidential reports, or to store sensitive information of any type, might find it advisable to format floppy disks to hold their data. Ability offers no password protection of any kind, so that anyone, who can gain access to the computer, can also access the files on the hard disk. The most secure way to store any data is to hold it on a floppy disk, locked in a safe when not in use.

The only exception is within Communicate, where you can set passwords to prevent distant users from copying your files down the telephone lines.

■ SECTION 2
Before you start

Installing Ability

With some packages there is a special installation program, which is used to customise the software to suit your particular computer system. Ability does not have such a program. Instead, it has a routine within the main system, for selecting printer and plotter types, and screen colours. But before you can use it, of course, you have to get Ability up and running.

■ SECTION 3

Getting going

While Ability can be run successfully on a double-floppy drive system, and even – with a little more effort – on a single drive machine, it does assume that it is being used with a hard disk, and that all data will be stored there. So, with a hard disk system, simply change to the Ability directory and start the program by typing '**ability**'. That's all there is to it. The program will load in, and your data files will be to hand.

You can start up on a floppy system in much the same way. That is, put the system disk into the A: drive and type '**ability**'. Then, when prompted, replace this with the help disk. But if you do this, Ability will assume that your data files are in the C: drive.

This does not create a major problem, as you can switch drives from within the program. (See below.) However, it is quicker and easier to start as you mean to go on.

Start with the Right Drive

On a double floppy system, the data files should be stored on a disk in the B: drive. Get the program running from MS-DOS by typing:

A> ability b:

On a single floppy system the data disk will be in drive A:. Start up with:

A> ability a:

With a hard disk, if you want to keep data on a floppy in A:, use:

C> ability a:

However you start the program, you will be presented with the title page, and then, at a touch of the spacebar, reach the Library screen. We will look at this very important part of the software shortly. For the moment, let's concentrate on one small part of it.

Switching Drives

If you forget to include the data drive letter in the command line, and it is easily done, you can switch drives while the program is running. This is done through the Library screen.

Getting going

At the bottom of the screen you will see a reminder of the facilities that can be called up by pressing the function keys. Only four of them are active in the Library.

```
F1 — Help                                    F9  — Flip
F2 — Commands                                F10 — Done
```

Press **[F2]** to call up the selection of commands. You will see this list appear at the bottom of the screen:

```
[Put-away] Active-drive Directory Erase Rename Copy File-stats
Other
```

The one that you want is 'active-drive'. Press **[A]** to select this, or use the pointing method. Move the highlight bar onto this with the cursor keys. The message 'Change the disk drive' will pop up on the line beneath. Select this command by pressing **[Enter]**. You will then be presented with a choice of drive letters, and the current one will be highlighted:

A: B: [C:]

Move the highlight to the one you want to use, and press **[Enter]**. Alternatively, select the drive by typing its letter.

The system will grind for a few moments while Ability gears itself up to using the new drive, and then you will be back to the Library screen.

■ SECTION 4
Your own devices

You should only need to perform this routine once, but do it before you start to tackle any real work with Ability. You are going to tell Ability about your printer, plotter and monitor.

As every new user is going to have to tackle the devices routine, they might have made it a bit more obvious to find. But they didn't.

Press **[F2]** to call up the commands, as you would to change drives. 'devices' is not included in the display, but notice that heading at the right-hand end – 'other'. Select this, either by moving the highlight bar and pressing **[Enter]**, or by pressing its initial **[O]**.

```
Print   Snapshot   Macros  [Devices] Run  Use-DOS
View/change printer,plotter,modem or screen color
```

A new menu is shown, and in this you will find 'devices'. Move along to it, and the comment line will tell you what it is supposed to do. Ignore the mention of the modem, as this cannot be controlled by the devices routine.

```
                   Printer, Plotter and Screen Color
                   ---------------------------------

Printer [Epson_FX]   Printer Port      [LPT1]   Printer Flow Control [XON/XOFF]
                     Printer Baud Rate [1200]
                     Page Width        [8.5 ]
                     Page Depth        [11  ]

Plotter [HP2pen  ]   Plotter port      [COM1]   Plotter Flow Control [XON/XOFF]
                     Plotter Baud Rate [████]

Country [UK     ]

Normal Screen color [Lt Green ]
"Flip" Screen color [Lt Cyan  ]
Screen mode         [Graphic  ]

View or change printer, plotter or screen color                    93% Free

F1 - Help                                                          F10 - Done
```

FIGURE 4-1 The Devices screen

■ SECTION 4
Your own devices

The screen shows the current settings of all the devices. There is quite a lot of information, but fortunately much of it can be safely ignored most of the time. If you want to change any setting, the method is almost always the same.

Move the cursor to the item you want to change.
Press **[Enter]** to bring an alternative setting into view.
Keep pressing until you reach the right one.
Move on to the next item, or quit by pressing **[Esc]** or **[F10]**.

Printers

The most likely thing that you will want to change is the name of your printer. Most of the commonly used printer names are there, and if you cannot see yours, the chances are that it is either Epson or IBM compatible, so select one of those instead. (The Epson FX standard will work perfectly well with a great many different printers.)

While you are in the printer section, check that the page width and depth is right for your paper. To change these settings, type in the new values. A4 – the most popular size for single sheet paper – is 8.25 by 11.75 inches; continuous stationery is generally 8.5 by 11 inches.

Screen Colours

If you have a colour monitor, go to the 'normal screen color' box and cycle through the available colours. As you do so, the screen colour will change to match the setting. Stop when you find one that you like.

The background colour will always be black, but the foreground colour – the one used for the text – can be any of the 16 available colours in the PC's palette. The default colour is light green, which can be a bit tiring on the eyes after a while. I prefer light cyan or white.

■ SECTION 4
Your own devices

There is a second screen colour, because Ability lets you work on two screens at a time, using the flip facility. With this, you can leave one part of the software, do some other work elsewhere in the system, then return to where you were before. So, in the middle of writing a letter, you could go across to the Database to get some information, then go back and finish the letter. The flip screen can be displayed in a different colour, as a reminder of where you are.

Screen Mode

There are only two options here – **graphics** and **text**. You must select graphics if you want to use the Graph facilities. The text option gives slightly faster screen handling, and may be useful where Ability is being used mainly for word-processing.

Exit from the devices screen by pressing **[Esc]** or **[F10]**. The new settings will be saved on disk and read back in whenever Ability is used again. If you need to change them at any time, you can always repeat the process.

■ SECTION 5
The Library

This is the central part of the software, so an understanding of what is going on here is crucial. Let's take a trip around the screen.

```
                 <<<<    Ability Plus v1.0   >>>>

DATABASE   SPREADSHEET  GRAPH      WRITE     COMMUNICATE  PROGRAMS     FILES

<<New>>      <<New>>    <<New>>    <<New>>     <<New>>     COMMAND        [A:]
REQUESTS     CASHFLOW   BAR1       MACROPG      TECH       DRIVERS        [B:]
STOCK        CUDDLES    BAR2       MARCHRPT     WAVE       MEMO           [C:]
STOCK2       EMACS      CASHGRAF   PRACTICE                PRESENT        [D:]
             INCOME     PROFITS                           SHOW           <..>
             MACS       SOFT1                                         ABILITY.ARC
             REVENUE    SOFT2                                         CONFIG.SYS
             RISES      SOFT3                                            DEMO.SNA
             TAHITI     SOFT4                                         PRESENT.HLP
             TITLEDEM   SOFT5                                          SNAPS.SNA
                        SOFT6




C:\ABILITY                                              28% Free
Please point at a file with ←↑↓→ and press ⏎
F1 - Help        F3 - Goto      F5 - Pick Up               F9 - Flip
F2 - Commands                                              F10 - Done
```

FIGURE 5-1 The Library screen

It might help at this stage if you have a disk with some Ability files on it in the data drive. The Presentation disk will serve very well. Slot it into the drive, then press **[F2]** to access the commands; select active-drive, and type the drive letter. This will make Ability check the disk to see what files are on it.

■ SECTION 5
The Library

The File Display

The middle section of the screen shows the files that are stored on the data disk, or in the current directory. They are arranged by type and listed under the appropriate heading. Ability can tell which file belongs to which part of the system because it stores them with a special type extension. If you look at them closely, using Ability's file-stat command, you will see that the word-processed files all have '.XTX' (TeXt) at the end of their names; Spreadsheet files have the extension '.XSS' (Spreadsheet); Graph files are marked '.XGR', and so on. These extensions do not appear on the screen, but you may need to use them when tidying up your disk storage, or when exchanging files with another Ability user over the telephone line.

Ability takes a somewhat unusual, but very effective, approach to work. You might have expected that when you wanted to do some word-processing, you would first select the Write option, and then, when that was running, pick from a list of existing text files or give the name of a new one. But Ability does not work that way. To use Write with an existing file, you simply move the cursor to its name (in the Write list), and press **[Enter]**. To Write a new file, point to the <<**NEW**>> label at the top of the Write list, press **[Enter]**, then type the name that you will use.

It is all part of the integration. When you want to start work on a file, you must be able to see what other files are on the disk, as Ability allows you to move data freely between files in different parts of the system.

Naming Files

The names that you give to your files must follow certain rules:

No more than eight characters may be used.
Any combination of letters or digits is permitted.
Punctuation signs and spaces are NOT allowed.
The underscore or hypen can be used to break up a name.
Upper or lower case letters may be used – the system will capitalise all names.

These are the rules set by the system. There is another which is every bit as important:

Make the name meaningful!

Give a file a cryptic name and you will have totally forgotten what it contained when you come back to it after a few weeks.

Here are some examples of good, bad and impossible filenames:

```
BANK ACC              Illegal, contains space.
BANK_ACC                   That's better!
DOC.23            Illegal, contains full stop.
DOC-23         Usable, but what was it?
tax87-88          Ah, so that's what it was.
Sales-October              Too long.
Octsales               That'll do nicely
```

The Status Line

```
Write: SALESREP        Page 2  Line 22  Col 29      89% Free
```

This highlighted strip will be found across the bottom of the working screen in all parts of the Ability system. Basically, it tells you where you are and what you are doing. On the left-hand side it will always show the amount of free space left in memory; and the CAPS and NUM indicators will appear here if the appropriate lock keys are pressed. In the Library, it also shows the current data drive or directory, on the right-hand side.

The Function Keys

```
F1 — Help                                          F9 — Flip
F2 — Commands                                      F10 — Done
```

Wherever you are in the Ability system, the bottom of the screen will always display a reminder of the facilities that are available from the function keys. Each key always serves the same, or very similar, purposes, but not all of the keys are active at all times. When you are in the Library, only four keys are active.

■ SECTION 5
The Library

[F1] – *Help*
The help facilities are always at hand, though you must have the
ABILITY.HLP file on the disk in the data drive if they are to work.
The pages that are displayed will depend upon the context within
which you asked for help. On the Library screen, the help pages
will tell you about using the Library. If you are about to select a
command in the Spreadsheet module, the help page will be about
that command.

[F2] – *Commands*
If you have been through either the disk switching or device
setting routines, you will already have met this. To select a
command from any line menu, either point the cursor at the
command name and press **[Enter]**; or press the initial letter of the
name. The pointing method is more informative – Ability gives a
brief description of the highlighted command on the line below
the menu. Typing the initial is quicker.

[F2] is always active, though the commands that it calls up will
depend upon which part of the system you are in. In the Library,
the commands are mainly concerned with file and disk management. They are quite extensive and are covered in the next three
sections.

[F9] – *Flip*
Ability has a limited, but very useful, multi-tasking facility. You
can have two files open at the same time and switch easily from
work on one to work on the other. Press **[F9]** and your current
operation will be suspended, the screen colour will change, and
you can start a new task. Press **[F9]** again, and the second task will
be suspended while you return to the first. It is a facility which has
proved of great value when writing this book, as it has enabled me
to create illustrations and check operations while working on the
text.

[F10] – *Done*
Press this at the end of any operation to signal that you have
finished. Ability will then take care of any house-keeping that
needs doing. Press it at the end of writing a letter or building a
spreadsheet, and the file will be saved as you are returned to the
Library screen. Press it within the Library screen when you want
to end the working session – Ability will check that you really want
to return to DOS, just in case it was pressed by mistake.

■ SECTION 6
The disk and directory commands

Active-drive

Select the drive which contains the data disk. You must use this if you ever change the data disk during a working session, even although you are still using the same drive. The command makes Ability look at the disk in the chosen drive and take a note of the names of the files that are stored there. Note that you cannot change disks if you are currently working on a file in the data drive, and that on a double-floppy system, you cannot use the A: drive as the active drive. This must contain the Ability disk.

Directory

The facilities available under this heading are probably only of relevance to hard-disk users. True, you can create directories on a floppy disk, but there is normally little purpose.

Floppy disks do not hold that much data, and they are so cheap that it is scarcely worth the effort of sub-dividing them. The Library screen will, in any case, sort them into type, so that even if there are 30 or 40 files in total, there will be only a limited number in each list. Use a new disk for each related set of files, and label the disk clearly. Do that, and you can forget all about directories.

The situation is very different on a hard disk. There you may easily have hundreds of different files, which makes locating any particular file about as easy as finding the proverbial needle in a haystack. A well-organised directory structure, with files grouped by type, makes it much easier to find what you are looking for.

Some people create structures of almost Byzantine complexity on their hard disks. It really is not necessary, and may well be self-defeating as the object of directories is to make file-handling easier. Keep things simple.

Create separate sub-directories within the Ability directory for each related set of files. Do not bother about organising the Ability program files into a directory, as once the program is up and running, you do not need to do anything with these. When a directory starts to get too full, you have two choices. Either you can create a further sub-directory within it, or you can make a new directory at the same level. I prefer the second option. That way, all of your data directories will be immediately visible from the same Library screen.

■ SECTION 6
The disk and directory commands

There are three options under the Directory heading:

Make-directory creates a new directory. this will be fitted into the structure as a sub-division of the current directory. Assume that you are working to the structure shown in Figure 6.1. When you first start, the status line will show that you are working in the \ABILITY directory. Select the make-directory option and give the name 'SALES87', to create the first data directory. Later, when you are working within \SALES87 and want to create somewhere to hold the next year's sales data, change back to the \ABILITY level, and make the directory from there.

The rules for naming directories are the same as those for naming files. Essentially, the name can be any combination of up to eight letters and digits.

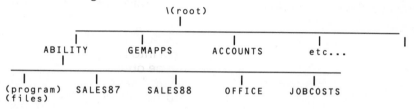

FIGURE 6-1 Make-directory

Change-directory allows movement between directories. The conventions that are used here are more obvious with a sub-divided structure, as shown in Figure 6.2.

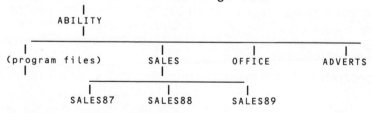

FIGURE 6-2 Change-directory

When you are going down a level – to a sub-directory – just give the directory name. So, to change from \SALES to \SALES88, type **'SALES88'**.

The disk and directory commands

To move across at the same level, or to go up to a higher level, you must give a backslash in front of the name. Thus, if you have been working in \SALES88, you would need to type **\SALES87**, **\SALES** or **\OFFICE** to reach any of those directories.

If you want to move across and down a level, you need to give the whole of the 'path name' – that is, the names of the directories that you are passing through, separated by backslashes. To get from the \OFFICE down to \SALES88, you would need to give the name **\SALES \SALES88**. As this can get complicated, leaving lots of room for typing errors, it is often simpler to change directories one stage at a time.

Remove-directory gets rid of unwanted directories. These must be empty before they can be removed. If there are any files present, Erase them first.

■ SECTION 7
File management commands

Put-away

When you are working on a file, Ability keeps a copy of it in its memory as well as on disk. This copy remains there even after you stop work on that file and start on another. At any one time there could be several separate files, all held in memory. The ones that are stored in this way are displayed with an asterisk after their names. This technique allows you to get data from files much quicker than you could if they were only on the disk, but you can run out of space.

Use put-away to clear the files that are no longer in active use. There are two options:

> This-one – remove the highlighted file only.
> All   – remove all starred files from memory.

Before you call up any of these next four commands, move the highlight bar to the name of the file that you want to work on. You cannot select a file from within the command routines.

Erase

When you select Erase, Ability will check that you really mean it – type **[N]** for No if you have any doubts. It is difficult, and sometimes impossible, to recover a file that was erased by mistake.

Rename

Use this to change the name of the current (highlighted) file. Ability will prompt you for the new name, and the usual rules apply. You cannot use this, or any, command for renaming directories.

■ SECTION 7
File management commands

Copy

This command is mainly used for creating back-up copies of files, and, where there is a directory structure, for copying files across to another directory for use there. The name of the copy must be different from the original, unless it is to be stored in a new directory. In this latter case, the name must include the directory. e.g.

```
JUNESUM    copied to    JUNESUM2              (Back-up)
JUNESUM    copied to    ACCOUNTS\JUNESUM      (new directory)
```

File-stats

This gives you the same information about a file as the MS-DOS DIR command: its name, size and time of last alteration. Note that you get the full name, with the type extension. A very useful byproduct of this command is that you can see how much space is left on the disk.
e.g.

Name is MAYSUM.XSS, size is 9,056 bytes, modified on 3-4-88 at 3.45pm
158,034 bytes available on disk

■ SECTION 8
The Other commands

Other calls up a second set of commands:

Print

Use this to print the current (highlighted) file onto paper. Its operation will vary slightly depending upon the type of files to be printed. The main features are described in full in the word-processing section, and variations are covered within the sections on the Spreadsheet, Graph and Database.

Snapshot

This turns on the screen-grabbing function that you need to build a file of pictures for a presentation. Once activated, Ability will take a 'snapshot' of the screen and add it to your picture file every time you press the large [+] key on the right side of the keyboard. (By the way, that [+] key is always used for taking snapshots – whether the 'camera' is loaded or not. You cannot use it for addition.) Snapshots and presentations are covered at the end of the book.

Macros

Ability allows you to set up two-key combinations, e.g. [Alt] – **[F1]**, or [Shift] – **[F5]**, so that by pressing them you can call up a chunk of text or a series of command keystrokes. This useful time-saving facility is covered fully in Section 48.

Devices

You met this command already, in Section 4, when installing your printer and selecting your screen colours.

Run

In theory, this allows you to run any other MS-DOS program from within Ability. It might be more accurate to say that this allows you to start up another program, or give a DOS command, from within Ability, then eases the return afterwards. In practice, it is of limited value. You have to get the right disks in the right drives at the right times; you have to wait while Ability reloads on return; and the method will not work with some software.

■ SECTION 8
The Other commands

The function's main use may be in running the occasional DOS utility and WKS, the special Ability program that translates Lotus 1-2-3 WorKSheet files into Ability Spreadsheet files.

1 Slot the disk containing the required program into your data drive and give the Active-drive command, or change to the program's directory.

2 Highlight the program name.

3 Select **[F2]** – Other – Run.

4 Type the program's name, or press **[Enter]** to pick the current file.

5 You will sometimes be prompted for 'the remainder of the command line'. If you were using the DOS Diskcopy to make a backup disk, the command might normally be typed in as **DISKCOPY A: B:**. Using Run, you have got the **DISKCOPY** already, all that needs to be added is **A: B:**. Some programs need no more than their name. For these, just press **[Enter]** at the prompt.

6 On a floppy disk system, make sure that the Ability system disk is in drive A: when the other program ends.

Use-DOS

This is a variation on **Run**, to be used when you want to perform several DOS functions before returning to Ability. On a floppy disk system, place the MS-DOS system disk in your active drive before calling it up, and have the Ability system disk in drive A: when you are finished.

You are supposed to be able to signal that you have finished with DOS and want to return to Ability by typing **exit**. This does not always seem to work, and you may have to restart with **ability** in the usual way.

PART TWO

Word Processing

■ SECTION 9
Write typing and typewriting

If you are an extremely accurate typist and highly organised in what you write, then Write holds few advantages over the common typewriter. If, on the other hand, you belong to that larger section of humanity who make mistakes and do not always plan everything properly first, word processing pays real dividends. Even if you are accurate and organised, using Write can still save time and energy, for you can copy and reuse text, so that you never have to type the same thing twice.

The real difference between using Write and using a typewriter is in the ability to edit text. At any point, you can stop what you are writing and go back to correct a mistake, insert, delete, copy or move a word, phrase or block of any size. Write also gives you a high degree of control over the final appearance of the printed text, both in its layout and in the choice of typefaces. Write uses a WYSIWYG display – What You See Is What You Get. Being able to see exactly how and where text will appear on the page, and particularly whether or not you have an awkward paragraph break at the bottom of a page, is a great help in producing a good printed output.

The width and length of pages can be altered at any time before, during or after you have written the text. It will automatically be reformatted to fit into the new size. Text is normally aligned to the left, with the right side 'ragged', but there are several variations on this. You can indent a paragraph, so that all its lines are set in from the left edge; the right side can be neatly aligned, by turning the justification option on; and for special headings or titles, lines can be centred on the page. Lastly, you can access the type options available from your printer, selecting draft or near letter quality print, Condensed, Elite or Pica typefaces, and picking out items within the text by the use of **bold**, *italics* and underlining.

It takes a bit of time and practice to really get the best out of Write, but you can still do a lot of useful work if all you know is how to type, move around the text and make simple corrections.

■ SECTION 10
Starting to Write

To start a new file, move the cursor to <<NEW>> in the Write column of the Library screen and press **[Enter]**. You will be asked for the name. Remember the eight-letter maximum!

To edit an existing file, point to its name and press **[Enter]**.

The Write Screen

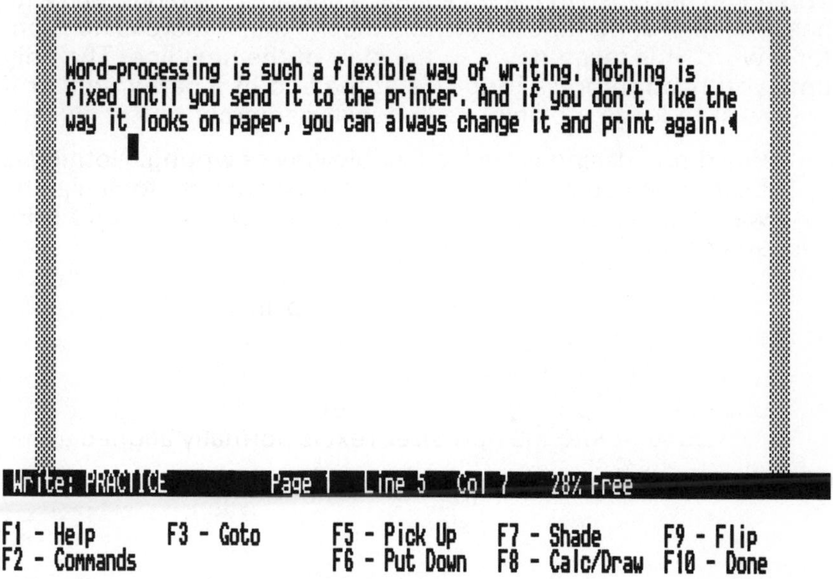

```
Word-processing is such a flexible way of writing. Nothing is
fixed until you send it to the printer. And if you don't like the
way it looks on paper, you can always change it and print again.◀
    ▮
```

Write: PRACTICE	Page 1	Line 5	Col 7	28% Free

F1 - Help	F3 - Goto	F5 - Pick Up	F7 - Shade	F9 - Flip
F2 - Commands		F6 - Put Down	F8 - Calc/Draw	F10 - Done

FIGURE 10-1 The Write screen

The working part of the screen occupies the top 21 lines. The half-tone border forms the outline of each page – the bottom line will be found a couple of screens down. Its size can be changed by altering the left and right margins and the page length. The page layout controls are part of the command set, and we will return to them later.

On the **status line** you will see the name of the current file on the left and the usual free memory and CAPS and NUM indicators on the right. In between are the page, line and column numbers of the cursor position. Keep an eye on these as you test the cursor movement keys.

■ SECTION 10
Starting to Write

Nine of the ten **function keys** are active at all times in Write. The tenth can also be brought into play. But before we can really see the effect of any of these, or of the cursor keys, we need some text.

Type in some text — you might like to use the following sample. If you make a mistake, use the backspace key [<-Del] to rub it out. When you get close to the end of each line, just keep typing. Write has a wrap-around function, which means that if there is no room for a word, it is taken down to the start of the next line. The only time you need to press **[Enter]** is at the end of a paragraph, or if you want to leave a blank line between paragraphs.

Word-processing is such a flexible way of writing. Nothing is fixed until you send it to the printer. And if you don't like the way it looks on paper, you can always change it and print again.

■ SECTION 11
Cursor movement

The simplest way to move the cursor is with the special cursor keys. (Figure 11.1). Notice that the **[PgUp]** and **[PgDn]** keys are used to move a screen 'page', or 21 lines, at a time; and that **[Home]** and **[End]** move only to the ends of the line.

```
Start of Line      1 Line Up      1 Screen Up
                                    (21 lines)
              [Home] [ ↑ ] [PgUp]
1 character Left-[ ← ] [   ] [ → ] -- 1 character Right
              [End ] [ ↓ ] [PgDn]
   End of Line       1 Line Down    1 Screen Down
                                    (21 lines)
```

FIGURE 11-1 Cursor keys

If you hold the **[Ctrl]** key while you press them, most will give bigger movements. (Figure 11.2) There are no fast ways of moving up and down within a screen. **[Ctrl]** + **[PgUp]** takes you to the top of the current page, or to the top of the previous page if you are already at Line 1, Column 1.

```
Start of Text      No Effect      Top of (Previous) Page
              [Home] [ ↑ ] [PgUp]
Start of Previous [ ← ] [   ] [ → ] -- Start of Next Word
   Word
              [End ] [ ↓ ] [PgDn] End   ↓   PgDn
   End of Text      No Effect      Top of Next Page
```

FIGURE 11-2 [Ctrl] and cursor keys

Where the cursor keys are combined in the number keypad, they cannot be used when the NUM lock is on, except by pressing **[shift]**. Even then, the **[Ctrl]** + **[shift]** + key combinations do not all work properly. At these times, it may be more convenient to use that cluster of keys on the left-hand side of the keyboard, which also gives control over the cursor. (Figure 11.3)

Cursor movement

```
Top of (Previous) Page      1 Line Up   1 Screen Up
                                        (21 lines)
                      [ Q ] [ W ] [ E ] [ R ]
1 character Left  --------             ---------- 1 character Right

Start of Previous- [ A ] [ S ] [ D ] [ F ]-- Start of Next Word
      Word
                      [ Z ] [ X ] [ C ]

  Top of Next Page         1 Line Down  1 Screen Down
                                        (21 lines)
```

FIGURE 11-3 [Ctrl] and letter keys

The TAB Key

One quick way to hop along a line is to use the tab key – the one with the two arrows, next to **[Q]**. Press it, and the cursor will jump to the next tab setting on the right; press **[shift]** and **[tab]** and it will jump to the tab setting to the left. The tab facility is there, as on a typewriter, to make it easier to create tables of data. The stopping points are initially on every eighth column, but can be set anywhere you want. We will see how in Section 17.

Mouse Control?

If the DOS MOUSE.COM program has been run before Ability is loaded in, then you can use the mouse to control the cursor – if you have got very steady hands and a good, tame mouse. Generally, its use is not recommended as it tends to go too far, too fast.

■ SECTION 12
Making corrections

Overtyping

Sometimes the simplest way to correct, or to replace a word or phrase is by **overtyping**. This is particularly the case where you have miskeyed so that characters appear in the wrong order – I wish I had 5p for every time I have typed 'nmae' rather than 'name'! Just move the cursor to the error and retype. You might like to try it by replacing 'flexible' with 'friendly' in the sample text. The two words are exactly the same length, so no other editing is needed.

> Word processing is such a **friendly** way of writing. Nothing is fixed until you send it to the printer. And if you don't like the way it looks on paper, you can always change it and print again.

Inserting

To **insert** anything new into the text – whether it is a character, word or larger chunk of text – press the **[Ins]** key. This is a 'toggle' key, switching between insert and overtype modes. When insert is turned on, the text splits at the cursor, with the rest of the line to the right dropping down out of the way and the cursor changing from a simple rectangle to a double-ended arrow. Try it by inserting 'a letter or report' at the end of the first sentence.

Place the cursor on the full stop and press **[Ins]** to open up a space.

> Word processing is such a **friendly** way of writing
> . Nothing is
> fixed until you send it to the printer. And if you don't like the way it looks on paper, you can always change it and print again.

Type the new material, then press **[Ins]** to toggle Insert off. The text will close up and reformat into a neat paragraph.

> Word processing is such a **friendly** way of writing a letter or report. Nothing is fixed until you send it to the printer. And if you don't like the way it looks on paper, you can always change it and print again.

■ SECTION 12
Making corrections

Automatic Inserts

For some reason best known to itself, Ability automatically starts to insert if you overtype at the end of a line. This can be quite useful at times, but not if you are trying to rewrite a phrase that spans two lines. If you do not want to insert, turn it off by pressing the **[Ins]** key.

Deleting Text

To delete **single characters** use either **[<-Del]** (backspace), which deletes to the left of the cursor; or **[.Del]** on the number keypad, which deletes beneath the cursor.

If you want to delete more than a few characters, then you should use the **shade** facility – which brings us to the Function keys.

■ SECTION 13
The Write function keys

All the function keys have a purpose in Write – even **[F4]**, which is not normally included in the 'active' list, comes into play when you start to use fields. Three of the keys are exactly the same here as they are in the Library screen and elsewhere in the system:

[F1] – help, that useful source of reminders.
[F9] – flip, to get out of Write temporarily, so that you can do another job.
[F10] – done, to save the text to disk and return to the Library.

A further four keys are used in much the same way here as in the Spreadsheet and Database modules. Three of these are concerned with the manipulation of blocks of data:

[F5] – pick up, which stores a block in memory.
[F6] – put down, to copy a block to a new place.
[F7] – shade, used for defining blocks.

These three will be covered in the next section. The fourth, **[F8]** – calc/draw, is used to calculate the values held by fields. This can be left until later. First,let us concentrate on those two keys whose functions are specific to Write.

[F2] – Commands

Field Spreadsheet Graph Indent Center Typestyle Print Other

Page-format File Quit

Most of these commands offer quite extensive possibilities and are covered at length in later sections. What follows is largely a summary.

The Write function keys

Field

For anyone who has been brought up on common or garden word-processors, these next three commands are amazing. **Field** allows you to embed a variable into the text, and that variable can contain anything – word or phrase, number or calculation. At the very least, it means that you can create an invoice and get Write to work out the totals and the VAT for you. How many word processors can do that? But what is perhaps even more significant is that you can give that field a name and then use its data in another part of the system; and *vice versa*, you can bring data from a named field in a Spreadsheet or Database file into a field within Write.

The field concept is central to the way Ability works, and we will meet it time and again as we go round the other parts of the system.

Spreadsheet and Graph

Call these up and you can create a spreadsheet or a graph inside a Write document. The full range of facilities is there, just as if you had started work from the Library screen. The only difference is that, when you finish, you will return to Write, and the table or graph that you have created will be part of your text. We will return to this in Section 37, after we have looked at spreadsheets and graphs.

Indent

Indenting a paragraph is a good way to make it stand out from the body of the text. To do it, move the cursor as far in from the left as you want, press **[F2]** and select Indent.

> You can indent before you write the paragraph, or afterwards – the text will be reformatted to fit the new line width; and you can indent as far in from the left as you like.

Note that the effect only lasts until the end of a paragraph.

■ SECTION 13
The Write function keys

Center and Typestyle

To use these presentation commands, you must first mark off an area with [F7]-shade. We will return to these two in the next section.

Other – Page-format

This has a number of options, all concerned with the size and appearance of the page, and will be covered in the section on page layout.

Other – File

There are two options here:

File Load

The file load command lets you merge a text file from the disk into the current text. The new file will be inserted at the cursor position – although any block of text can always be moved easily, as you wil see when we look at **shade**.

This facility can be a great time-saver when you need to produce business letters or legal documents where you are writing much the same kind of thing time and again. A bank of standard paragraphs can be written once, and stored on disk either singly or in related sets. When you are creating a new document, the required paragraphs can be loaded in far more quickly than they could be typed.

A point to note here is that the routine does not give you any opportunity to check the names of the files on the disk. You must know what it is you want to load, before you use this command.

File Save

Your text file will be saved when you press [F10] to exit from Write, but, in a long session, it is always as well to use the file save option from time to time while you are working on a document. It will create a new version of the file on the disk, so that, should something disastrous occur, you will not lose too much work. Ability is a reliable piece of software, but accidents do happen. Power failures are rare, but possible; mains leads get tripped over; text can be deleted by mistake. It is always as well to have a reasonably up-to-date copy to fall back on.

You can give the file a new name before you save it, if you like, or continue to use its existing name. Note that when you save a file it will overwrite any other file on the disk that bears the same name, so a little care is needed in this respect.

Other – Quit

This ends the Write session without saving the file. It can be useful where you have been editing a file and have decided that it was a bad session and you preferred the earlier version; or where you have written and printed a memo or letter and do not want to clutter up the disk with an unnecessary copy.

■ SECTION 14
Search and replace

[F3] – Goto

There's more to this function key than first meets the eye. Of its two options **find-pattern** and **page**, the simplest is page. Select that, type the number of the page to which you want to go, and the cursor will leap to the top left corner of the desired page. It is a quick way of getting around a long file.

Find-pattern has two sub-options of its own:

Search

This is used when you want to track down a particular word or phrase – it may be a heading, or a key item in a section that you want to edit. You know it is somewhere in the text, but not on which page, so the **goto page** option is not appropriate.

It is sometimes best to leap up to the start of the file before beginning the search, but it does not really matter where you are in the text, the routine can look backwards as well as forwards.

```
                    Search for: "Spring Sales"
Next    Previous
Search forward for pattern              F1 - Help; Esc - Continue
```

When prompted, type in the text to search for. It does not matter if you use lower or upper case letters; Ability ignores the case, so that the search pattern 'spring sales' will also find 'Spring Sales' and 'SPRING SALES'.

Now select the search direction. **Next** looks forward; **previous** looks back up towards the start. When a matching pattern is found, the containing text will be displayed on screen. At that point you can search for a further match, in either direction, or press **[Esc]** to continue with your normal editing.

If the search reaches the end of the text without finding the pattern, you will get a 'No more occurrences' message. Press **[Esc]** to exit, or send the search in the other direction.

Search and replace

Replace

There are two important differences here from the search option. The first is implicit in the name. With this command, you can find any or every occurrence of a word or phrase and **replace** it with a new piece of text. It might be used, for example, to change some specific details in a generalised report, or the personal details in a letter – although mail-merging (see Section 45) would more commonly be used for that.

The second difference is that this routine only works through the text one way. You must start at the top of the file, or at least somewhere before the text to be altered.

```
       Search for: "Jackson"        Replace with: "Jones"
Fix   Skip Remainder
Replace pattern found with new text    F1 - Help; Esc - Continue
```

Type in the find-pattern and the replacement text to start the search. When a match is found, you have four options:

Fix replaces the text at the cursor position, then carries on the search.

Skip leaves the original pattern unchanged, but continues to search.

Remainder replaces the current occurrence, and any more that it finds in the rest of the file.

[Esc] ends the routine without changing the found text.

■ SECTION 15
Shaded blocks

The use of shading, or highlighting, to define a block is fundamental to much of Ability, not just to Write. A block may consist of anything from a few characters up to several pages of text, and once defined by shading, a block can be given special treatment. In Write, a shaded block can be set in a different typeface, deleted, moved or copied within the text or to another part of the Ability system.

The **Shade** operations revolve around three function keys – **[F5]**, **[F6]** and **[F7]**.

To SHADE a block

Place the cursor at one end of the block to be marked out, then press **[F7]**. The 'shade an area' message will appear below the status line.

Move the cursor to spread the highlight over the text that you want to include in the block.

That's all there is to it – the block is now defined and ready to be used.

To COPY a block

Press **[F5]** – pick up. The highlighting will be turned off, but the text will have been stored in memory.

Move the cursor to where you want the copy, and press **[F6]** – put down. There will be a brief pause while Write reformats the text.

The block may be copied as many times as necessary. It will remain in memory until a new block is defined, even if you exit from Write or flip to a different part of the system. This means that you can pick up a block in one file and put it down in another.

To DELETE a block

Press the **[.Del]** key on the numberpad. Although removed from the screen and from the text file, the block is held in memory until a new one is defined.

■ SECTION 15
Shaded blocks

To MOVE a block

There are two ways of doing this – the efficient way, and the coward's way.

If you want to be efficient, delete the block then move the cursor to where you want it to be, and press **[F6]** – put down. As long as you do not define another block between the start and end of this process, there will be no problem.

If the thought of wiping out all your hard-typed, and much-needed words is too much for you – and it can be unnerving to delete a couple of pages of text – then try the 'better safe than sorry' approach.

Copy the block, as described above, then return to its original site in the file. Press **[F7]** *TWICE*, and the old block will be highlighted once more. It can now be deleted without qualms.

■ SECTION 16
Emphasising text

If you want to make a heading or a block of text stand out, there are several possibilities. All are tackled in the same way.

Move the cursor to the start of the text that you want to emphasise, press **[F7]** and shade the heading, word or block. Now press **[F2]** to call up the command menu. The two items we are interested in are **center** and **typestyle**.

```
            Select the center option to get this effect;
                with text centered on the screen.
        It will only be in the centre of the printed page,
            if the margins are the same width both sides.
```

There are four typestyle options, **bold**, *italics*, <u>word</u> underline and <u>solid underline</u>. They can be used individually, or *<u>in combination</u>* to produce a **variety** of *effects*. Add to this the usual choice of lower case or CAPITALS, and you can really make things **STAND OUT**.

Where you want to apply a combination of typestyle options, do not forget that you can recall that last shaded area by pressing **[F7]** twice.

All of these effects are visible on the screen, and should appear much as they do on the printed copy – always assuming that your printer can produce bold, italics and underlines. You will also find, when we come to explore printing, that you can select the type style for the whole document.

Page format

The page-format command, one of the 'other' ones on the **[F2]** menu, gives you control over the size and appearance of the printed page. And as Write is a WYSIWYG (What You See Is What You Get) system, this is reflected in the screen display.

The default settings – the values written in at the start by Ability – are as follows:

```
Page-length        54 lines per page
Left-margin        10th column
Right-margin       74th column
Justification      OFF - text ragged at right edge
Headers            None
Footers            None
Tabs               Every 8th column, starting at 1
```

Any new settings that you give will be saved along with the text, and will come into play when you next load the file.

Page-length

Typical continuous stationery is 11 inches long, allowing a maximum of 66 lines of type when using the normal ⅙th inch line spacing. A4 paper is slightly longer and can hold 70 lines of print. Whatever page length is set, the remaining lines will be divided evenly between top and bottom margins – although you can adjust the printed position of the text by the simple expedient of winding the printer carriage up or down.

Margins

The left and right margins can be set to any values between 0 and 250. That may seem a little generous, but a wide carriage printer using the Condensed typeface could fit nearly 200 characters on a line, and if the file is to be printed sideways (see next section), then very wide pages can be used.

Note that these margins are for the printed output. Whatever settings are used, they will affect only the width of the screen display, not its position – the screen 'page' is always centered.

Justification

When justification is turned ON, the spaces between words will be padded out so that the lines all stretch to the right margin, as they do in this book. While this usually looks neater than a ragged, unjustified edge, a combination of narrow pages and long words can produce some odd effects.

To Justify, or not to Justify, that is the question. Whether 'tis more readable and presentable to leave a ragged edge or to have words scattered and strewn by overspacing,	To Justify, or not to Justify, that is the question. Whether 'tis more readable and presentable to leave a ragged edge or to have words scattered and strewn by overspacing,

I leave it to you to decide, although as long as the page is at least 60 or so columns wide, overspacing should not be a problem. Unfortunately, there is no flexibility over justification. It is either ON or OFF for the whole text, and cannot be set otherwise for a single page or paragraph.

Headers and Footers

These are both set in exactly the same way. The only difference is that headers will be printed above the lines allocated to your text, and footers below. So, for the rest of this part, for 'headers', read 'headers or footers'. There are three decisions to make: where do you want them; what sort do you want; how should they be presented.

Where?

A header can be printed on the left, centre or right of the page, and you can have two or three if you want them. The **First-page** option allows you to leave the first page free of headers – useful if it is a title page.

What?

Headers can be of three types – text, page-number or date. The page numbering will always start at 1 when shown on the screen, although there is a facility in the print routine to start at any chosen value – an essential requirement if you have a set of related files that are to be numbered consecutively.

■ SECTION 17
Page format

The date is today's date, as taken from the computer's internal clock and calendar. It cannot be altered, except by resetting that calendar.

How?

You cannot apply any of the **typestyle** options to the headers. When they are displayed on the screen they are outside of the box that encloses the working page, and so it simply is not possible to shade them. However, there are alternative forms of presentation.

Page numbers can be displayed in any of three ways:

```
Alone            with hyphens        with a page prefix
  6                 - 6 -                 Page 6
```

Dates can be shown in any of four different ways:

```
American        European         Metric           Long
03/29/88        29-03-1988       85-03-29      March 29, 1988
```

If you want to remove a header, select the text option and press **[Enter]** when prompted for the text.

By combining the different types of header, I get the following display along the top of each page of this current file:

```
Using Ability              - 16 -              March 29, 1988
```

Tabs

Whenever you need to create a neat table of figures, a few moments spent in setting tabs will make the writing much quicker.

Call up the tabs routine, and you will get a number line display with a succinct display of prompts. The 't's along the number line show the current tab positions; the figures are aligned by the second digit. At the '20', for example, '2' is on the 19th column, '0' on the 20th.

■ SECTION 17

Page format

The number line continues off the side of the screen, to the 250th column.

> t...5...t0...15.t.20...2t...30..t35...40t..45...t0...55.t.60...6t...70
>
> Press < , >, |<- , ->| Move cursor Set tab Erase tab Clear all tabs

To move the cursor along the line, either:
> single-step with the left/right cursor keys;
> jump to the next 't' with [tab] or [shift] + [tab];
> leap from end to end with [home] and [end].

> Press **[C]** to clear all tabs at once.
> Press **[E]** to erase a tab under the cursor.
> Press **[S]** to set a new tab at the cursor position.
> Press **[Esc]** when finished.

Do not forget that tab settings, as with all other aspects of the page format, are saved along with the text and will not need resetting next time round.

■ SECTION 18
Printing out

A file may be printed out at any time, whether it has been saved or not. Nor does it matter whether you call up the print routine from within Write, or from within the Library screen. They are identical, and are both to be found in the **[F2]** command sets.

```
Epson-LQ: First-#1, pica, entire file, continuous paper, draft copy
Go  To-file  First-page  Cpi  Range  Paper Sideways  Quality
```

Select **print**, and the prompts at the bottom of the screen will show you the current settings and the range of options. Check those settings, and check that your printer is ready. Then, if no changes are needed, press **[G]** or point to **go** to start the output.

Print Options

Printer Name

This *cannot* be changed from the print routine. It must be set by the **devices** command in the Library. When you select a printer name, you tell Ability which *driver* to use. This is a special sub-program that will convert Write's typestyle instructions into codes that the printer can understand.

The range of options shown in the print routine will depend upon the choice of printer. If it cannot produce letter quality printing, for example, the quality option will not be included.

First-page

If page-number is included in a header or footer, the numbering will start from 1 unless this option is used to set a different starting value.

Cpi

This controls the pitch – the number of characters per inch. The current setting will be shown by name rather than by number.

Pica is the normal pitch. At 10 cpi, this gives 80 characters across the usual 8-inch paper.

Elite produces a slim, but attractive typeface. It is useful where you need to get just a little extra on a line – perhaps to fit in a table that is a touch too wide. At 12 cpi, this can fit 96 characters across the width of a normal sheet.

56

Printing out

Condensed is best reserved for those times when capacity, not readability, is the key requirement. Depending upon the printer, this runs at 15 or 17 cpi – either 120 or 136 on a full page. If you need more than this, then use the Sideways option.

Range

Select the **pages** sub-option here if you want to print a limited set of pages. You will be asked for the numbers of the first and last page to include. Full pages are always printed. It is not possible to print a small set of lines, except by isolating those lines on an otherwise blank page.

Ability assumes that you will want to print all of the file. Even if you set a range, next time you select the Print command, the 'entire file' will be shown as the current setting. The **all** sub-option of **range** is only there in case you change your mind about the **pages** setting.

Paper

The choice here is between continuous fan-fold stationery and single sheets.

Sideways

This option is not available with some printers. It may well be of more use with spreadsheets than with text files, where you are far less likely to have width problems. You may occasionally want to use this option, however, even although the text would fit in the upright mode. The type is slightly larger and better spaced than normal, and would produce more readable notices.

Before using this, you should be aware of several things:

■ For reasons best known to Ability itself, the top two lines are not printed. Insert two dummy lines at the top to overcome this.

■ The characters are printed at about 8.5 cpi, giving almost 100 across the full depth of a page.

■ You will get 31 lines across the width of continuous stationery.

■ As the printer has to work harder, printing is significantly slower than normal.

Printing out

Select **sideways** from the sub-menu to turn this on; **upright** if you change your mind. When the **print** command is called up, the current setting will always be upright.

Quality

This option will only be offered if your printer has a near letter quality mode. Select **draft copy** where printer speed is more important than appearance; **final copy** for higher quality print.

Print Now or Later?

The printer is normally the second slowest part of the computer system. This is because it is a mechanical device with moving parts that are hampered by such things as inertia and friction. Memory access and screen displays suffer no such limitations, and even disk drives, which have mechanical components, are much faster. There is only one part of your computer system that is slower than the printer, and that is you!

If you have a long file that needs printing, but do not want to have to suspend all other work while the printer grinds away, the solution lies in the **to-file** option. Select this, then **disk** from the sub-menu. Press **[G]** for Go, and instead of being sent to the printer, the file will be written on the disk in a printable format. This is different from the normal text file storage in that it will contain the range, cpi, quality and other settings. The file can then be run off at the end of the session with the DOS PRINT command, or via the print spooler in the Gem system.

There can be few businesses that do not use some form of standard letters – reminders of outstanding bills, covering notes with deliveries, job quotations, announcements of special offers. Using Ability, you will no longer have to type each one out afresh; and the secret of this is the use of *fields*.

A field is a named place, in which any kind of data can be stored, or in which calculations can be made. In a spreadsheet, every cell is a field; in a database, each part of every record is a field. A text file is different, for the use of fields is entirely optional. If used, they may positioned anywhere.

Probably the best way to understand what a field is, and what it can do, is to see one in action. To take a simple example, we will get Ability to produce headed notepaper with today's date written into a field. It would be saved as a blank sheet, and loaded back in whenever you wanted to write a letter.

```
              Mr. & Mrs. D. Thatcher
                10 Downing Street
                     London
```

The name and address are written in as normal, then move the cursor to where you want the date, press **[F2]** to call up the commands, and select **field**. The prompt line at the bottom of the screen will show:

VALUE Enter field1: field1=0

Notice the two aspects of the field – its name and its contents. Ability has given this the name 'field1', but that can easily be changed to something more memorable if need be.

Whenever you create a new field it will always start with a value of 0, but you can write any text, number, calculation or function into it. We want this field to hold the current date, and to do that we will use the Ability function **TODAY** which will read the date off the computer's internal calendar.

■ SECTION 19
Fields for flexibility

Writing Functions

Functions can be written into any field, anywhere in the Ability system. As their main use will almost certainly be in spreadsheets, they are covered more fully in the next part of the book.

There are a couple of conventions about functions that must be observed. First, the word must be prefixed by a plus sign (+). If it is not, then Ability will treat it as normal text. Secondly, most functions carry out some form of calculation on one or more values, and these are given in brackets after the function name. For example, **COMPOUND(principal, interest, periods)** calculates the compound interest on a sum over time; **SQRT(number)** works out the square root. As a result, ALL functions must have brackets after them, even although, as in this case, the brackets are left empty.

So, bearing these conventions in mind, type +**TODAY()** in at the prompt line. Just type straight over 'field1=0':

VALUE Enter field1: +TODAY()

If you make a mistake, use [<-Del] to erase back to it. Do not try to use the cursor keys to edit the entry – they will simply move the cursor on the screen, and hence off your new field.

As you press **[Enter]** a number will appear in the field on the screen. It will be something like '32321'. That may not look much like a date to you, but it is in fact the number of days that have elapsed since the start of the twentieth century – which is how the computer keeps the date. Fortunately, the **edit** command provides us with a simple way to get this into a more readable form.

We will work straight through the process of formatting the date, then return in the next section to look at the full potential of the edit facilities.

Fields for flexibility

Formatting a Date

1 If you have moved the cursor off the field, go back to it, so that the prompt line reappears. Notice that there is a new addition to the function key reminders at the bottom of the screen.

2 Press **[F4]** – Edit Field.

3 From the sub-menu **Edit Format Width Name** select **Format**.

4 At the next menu, select **date**.

Money Commas Fixed Variable Scientific Percent Date Justify

5 The date options are exactly the same as when you are setting Headers and Footers. The Long format may be most appropriate. Choose this and the number will be displayed in a readable form immediately.

6 Press **[Esc]** TWICE to get back up through the two levels of menu.

7 If you want to centre the field, put the cursor on it and use the normal **[F2]** and Center command.

Mr. & Mrs. D. Thatcher
10 Downing Street
London

June 28, 1988

■ SECTION 20
Editing fields

Although here we are focusing on Write, the field-handling commands are virtually identical throughout the Ability system. With these you can **edit** the contents of a field, set the display **format**, fix the width allocated to it and give the field a **name**.

When the cursor is on a field, whether it is when the field is being created or when you go back to it later, **[F4]** – Edit Field is active. You will see that it is included in the Function Key reminders at the bottom of the screen. Press **[F4]** and you will get this sub-menu:

Edit Format Width Name

Edit

To change the contents of an existing field, you can either overwrite it, or select this option and edit it. When in edit mode, the following keys may be used:

```
[Left]   [Right] — move cursor along the line
[Home]   [End]   — move cursor to ends of line
[Ins]             — toggles Insert mode ON/OFF
```

Format

This determines how numbers are displayed on the screen. The effects of the alternatives can be seen by looking at the same numbers under different Formats.

Number as entered	123	1234.567	−12.3	0.2345
Money — Standard	123.00	1,234.57	−12.30	0.23
— Negative ()	123.00	1,234.57	(12.30)	0.23
Commas	123	1,234.567	−12.3	0.2345
Fixed {See Note}	23.0	1234.6	−12.3	0.2
Variable	123	1234.567	−12.3	0.2345
Scientific	1.23E2	1.234567E3	−1.23E1	2.345E−1
Percent	12300%	123456.7%	−1230%	23.45%

Note: The **fixed** option allows you to set the number of decimal places (between 0 and 12). Here, the display was fixed at 1 decimal place only.

Of the two remaining format options, **date** has been covered above in Sections 17 and 19; **justify** only becomes relevant when the field has had its width set by the **width** command. Then it will allow you to set the *number* against the left or right edge of the field. You can write text into a field, but you cannot justify it. Text will always be printed from the left side of a field.

■ SECTION 20
Editing fields

Width

In a normal text file, this option would not be used as it specifies a fixed width for the field. This could lead to an ugly gap if the field was embedded in text. Leave it to its own devices, and the field will be just as wide as it needs to be to display its contents in the right format.

The width setting is done visually. Press the right or left cursor keys to stretch or shrink the highlight bar until it is the required length. A bit of pre-planning comes in useful here as you cannot see the contents of the field, merely a blank highlight bar; nor is there any counter to tell you how many character spaces the field covers. So work out the width before you start, then count the key presses as you set the field. That will save having to repeat the command to make final adjustments.

Name

All fields have names. If you do not supply the name, the system will. Write automatically allocates the names 'field1', 'field2', and so on as you create new fields.

There are three ways in which you can name a field.

■ Use the **name** command. Call this up, and type in the name when prompted. This is perhaps the simplest method.

■ Type in the name along with the data when you create a new field. Note that as soon as you start to type, the 'field1=0' display will be erased, and you must include the '=' in your new line:

   VALUE field1: field1=0
   VALUE field1: sa   (as typing starts)
   VALUE field1: salestotal=299.95

■ Use the **edit** command, and edit the existing name. You can delete any surplus characters, or create extra space with the [Ins] toggle.

   VALUE field1: field1=299.95
   VALUE field1: salestotal=299.95

■ SECTION 20
Editing fields

However you write it, a name must conform to these conventions:

■ it may contain no more than 13 characters;

■ letters, digits and underscores may be used, but the first three characters must be either letters or underscores;

■ capitals and lower case letters are treated as the same;

■ no two fields in a file may share a name.

And don't forget to make it meaningful and memorable!

Using Named Fields

If a document contains the odd one or two individual fields, there is little point in naming them. The value of names is only seen when you include calculations in a file, or when you want to pass data from one file to another. Names provide the means to draw data into a formula, as we shall see in the next section; and for making links between files. We will return to this when we have explored rather more of the Ability system.

Calculated fields

For anyone reared on traditional word processors − if something that has only been around for a couple of decades can be called 'traditional' − it comes as a surprise that you can use Write to perform calculations. But you can, and there is no limit to the number or complexity of those calculations. You could produce invoices, estimates, statements of account or similar documents just by using fields, though, in practice, once you get beyond a certain number of calculations, it is easier to create a spreadsheet and incorporate that into the text file.

To see how these calculated fields work, let's have a look at the following letter, sent out by the Sales Director of International Robotics Inc. to a prospective customer. The firm likes to reply to all enquiries individually, and as prices tend to vary rapidly, VAT and credit rates need to be calculated afresh each time.

Dear Sir,

Thank you for your enquiry about the AUTOBUTLER domestic robot.

This item is priced at £25,000.00 (£28,750.00 inc. VAT at 15%). If preferred it may be purchased under our Easy-Way instalment plan, as detailed below.

```
Cash Price (inc. VAT)          28,750.00
Interest Rate (monthly)             1.5%
Term in Months                        36
Monthly Payments                1,039.38
Total Credit Price             37,417.73
```

There are nine fields in use here. Notice how the names of some fields are used in the formulae in other fields.

Name	Contents	Format	Display
type	AUTOBUTLER	−	AUTOBUTLER
price	25000	Money	£25,000.00
vatinc	+price+price*vat	Money	£28,750.00
vat	0.15	Percent	15%
cashprice	+vatinc	Money	£28,750.00
rate	0.2	Percent	20%
term	36	−	36
monthly	+PMT(vatinc,rate,term)	Money	£1,039.38
credit	+monthly*term	Money	£37,417.73

Some fields just store data, mainly for use in formulae elsewhere −'type', 'price', 'vat', 'rate' and 'term' are all examples of this.

■ SECTION 21
Calculated fields

The simplest type of formulae transfer values from one field to another. The first line of the credit calculations calls down the VAT inclusive price that was found earlier in the letter. Notice how the field name is prefixed by a plus sign:

cashprice=+vatinc

The next level of formulae uses the arithmetic operators. The values that are being processed may be given as numbers or drawn from fields. You can see this in the fields 'vatinc' and 'credit'.

vatinc=+price+price*vat

Ability's built-in functions offer a most convenient way to perform some of the most complex calculations. The one used here, **PMT**, calculates the regular payments needed to repay a capital sum and interest over a period of time.

+PMT(vatinc,rate,term)

Why Bother?

If you had to create these fields and their formulae every time you wrote a letter, it would scarcely be worth the effort. For a one-off calculation, a pocket calculator will always be quicker. But, of course, that is not the case. This same basic letter can be re-used time and again. All that the Sales Director will have to do is edit the contents of the type, price, vat, rate and term fields, but only where they have changed from their previous values.

PART THREE

Spreadsheets

■ SECTION 22
The uses of spreadsheets

Just as word processors are displacing typewriters from offices throughout the modern business world, so spreadsheets are displacing calculators — and for much the same reasons. A spreadsheet is a far more efficient way of handling numbers. No matter what type of number-crunching job you have to do, you will only need to sit down once and work out the calculations needed to perform it. When that structure of formulae exists, you can feed in new numbers and get results immediately without any further effort.

```
       A              |      B     |     C      |     D      |
 1|Details                 Price       Quantity    Amount
 2|Large Blue Gribbles     12.00          1          12.00
 3|Small Pink Gribbles      4.00          2           8.00
 4|Medium Green Gribbles    8.00          5          40.00
 5|Tiny Green Gribbels      2.00          5          10.00
 6|Huge Black Quibbles     20.00          2          40.00
 7|Little Yellow Quibbles   5.00         10          50.00
 8|Soft Furry Quibbles     10.00          2          20.00
 9|Blue Suede Trobbles     30.00          4         120.00
10|                                               ----------
11|                                 Sub-total        300.00
12|                     Discount at        10%        30.00
13|                                               ----------
14|                                 Total            270.00
15|                     VAT at             15%        40.50
16|                                               ----------
17|                                 Amount Due       310.50
```

FIGURE 22-1 Invoicing with Spreadsheet

At the simplest, the spreadsheet can be used as an invoicing tool. Written into it will be calculations to total up the item costs, work out discounts and VAT and give final totals. The basic model for this type of sheet is shown here. In use, the sales assistant will only need to type in the details, price and quantity of each item, and the discount percent — if it is different from the last time the sheet was used. All the calculations will then be performed by the sheet — we will look later at the formulae that are needed for this.

More complex spreadsheets can be used to assess the potential value of investments or to cost alternative scenarios. It is perhaps in providing answers to the *'What if...?'* questions that the power of the spreadsheet is best seen.

The uses of spreadsheets

Take this simplified example. A firm is negotiating with its workforce over wage increases. There are two ways in which it can compensate for the increase without affecting its overall profit; one is to increase productivity, the other is to raise prices. These three items – the percentage change in wages, price and production – are the variable factors in the equations. The spreadsheet illustrated in Figure 22.2 has been designed so that, by feeding in possible values for wage and price increases, it will calculate the improvements in productivity needed to achieve the same profit level. The calculations could all be performed by hand, but at what cost in time and effort! With a spreadsheet, a dozen different combinations can be tried in a matter of moments.

	A	B	C	D
1	Wage Increase?	20%		
2	Price Increase?	3%		
3	Productivity Up....	<CIRC>	18%	
4				
5	Materials	40.00	40.00	
6	Labour	60.00	72.00	
7	Unit Cost	100.00	112.00	
8				
9	Production	10,000	<CIRC>	11800
10				
11	Variable Costs	1,000,000.00	1,321,600.00	
12	Fixed Costs	300,000.00	300,000.00	
13	Total Costs	1,300,000.00	1,621,600.00	
14				
15	Unit Sale Price	150.00	154.50	
16	Sales Income	1,500,00.00	1,823,100.00	
17				
18	Profit	200,00.00	201,500.00	
19				

FIGURE 22-2 What if? calculations

The sheet will not, of course, tell management how great a wage increase to concede, or by how much to raise prices – these are both decisions that involve more than mere numbers – but it will give the information they need to make rational decisions.

The sheet and the screen

The spreadsheet is composed entirely of fields, arranged in a grid of rows and columns. It is theoretically enormous, and the screen can only show a very small part of it. Rumour has it that there are nearly 1,000 rows and over 700 columns – that is 50 screens deep and about 100 screens across – but I have never strayed that far from home! In practice, you could never actually fill all the fields with data – apart from anything else, the computer would run out of memory. However, the vast size does give a lot of flexibility; you can make your spreadsheets long and thin, short and wide, or well spread out with different sections of the sheet each allocated their own special area.

	A	B	C	D	E	F	G	H
1	Profit Forecasts							
2								
3		Jan	Feb	March	April	May	June	June
4								
5	Soft Toys	5000	5000	4500	4000	4000	5000	7000
6	Knitwear	2500	2500	2000	1000	1000	1000	2000
7	Beachwear	0	1000	2000	2500	3000	2500	1000
8	Total Sales	7500	8500	8500	7500	8000	8500	10000
9								
10	Materials	3375	3825	3825	3375	3600	3825	4500
11								
12	Gross Profit	4125	4675	4675	4125	4400	4675	5500
13								
14	Overheads	4800	5040	7040	4800	4920	7040	5400
15								
16	Net Profit	-675	-365	-2365	-675	-520	-2365	100
17								
18	Balance	2825	2460	95	-580	-1100	-3465	-3365
19								
20								

Spreadsheet: CUDDLES   26% Free

LABEL   Enter A3: Y

F1 - Help   F3 - Goto   F5 - Pick Up   F7 - Shade   F9 - Flip
F2 - Commands   F4 - Edit Field F6 - Put Down   F8 - Calc/Draw   F10 - Done

FIGURE 23-1 Cashflow forecasting

■ SECTION 23
The sheet and the screen

Fields are identified by their column letter and row number, starting from A1 at the top left. The column letters run initially from A to Z, then AA to AZ, BA to BZ and so on. If you care to hunt for it, you will find that the bottom right field is at ZZ9999!

Spreadsheet fields are the same as those everywhere else in the system. They may contain text, numbers or calculations; the numbers may be formatted as money, percent and so on, to make their purpose more obvious to the user; the width of the field may be adjusted — although the method of adjustment is slightly different from that found in Write; and they may be given names, in place of the column/row co-ordinates.

The *current field*, highlighted by the cursor, is the one through which data is entered into the sheet. You cannot write directly onto the sheet in the way that you write text in the word processor. Everything passes through the data entry line, below the main screen. This is so that the system can check the entry before including it in the sheet. Text and numbers will normally be passed straight across, but formulae will be tested to make sure that they are written correctly. If the spreadsheet finds an error, it will point it out to you — usually with a helpful suggestion.

Formulae must begin with a number, an arithmetic operator (+ − * /), or the @ sign. (I have used the plus sign throughout this book.) It is important to remember the prefix if the first item in the formula is a field reference, a name or a function.

The formulae may contain any valid combination of numbers, references and functions. Where a function operates on a range of fields, the range is defined by the references of its upper left and lower right squares. Typical formulae might be:

```
120 * 0.15            Simple number arithmetic
+B7 - B2 * B3         Arithmetic on field references
+SALES_TOTAL * VAT    Fields identified by names
+TOTAL(C3..C10)       Function operating on a range
```

Cursor movement is almost identical to that in Write:

the arrow keys move you one field at a time in any direction;
[PgUp] and [PgDn] leap up and down 20 rows;
[home] and [end] jump to the ends of the row.

■ SECTION 23
The sheet and the screen

```
     Start of Row        1 Row Up        1 Screen Up
                                           (21 lines)
                      [Home] [ ↑ ] [PgUp]
  1 Field Left --[  ← ] [   ] [ → ] -- 1 Field Right
                      [End ] [ ↓ ] [PgDn]
     End of Row        1 Row Down      1 Screen Down
                                           (21 lines)
```

FIGURE 23-2 Cursor keys

If [Ctrl] is held down:

> [Left] and [Right] arrows jump 7 columns left or right;
> [PgUp] jumps to top field in current column;
> [PgDn] jumps to lowest occupied cell in current colum;
> [Home] takes you to the top left field;
> [End] takes you to the field at the bottom right of the active sheet.

```
              [Ctrl] + Cursor Keys
     Goto A1        No Effect      Top of Column
                 [Home] [ ↑ ] [PgUp]
  7 Fields Left  [ ← ] [   ] [ → ] -- 7 Fields Right
                 [End ] [ ↓ ] [PgDn]
Bottom Right Corner  No Effect      Bottom of Column
```

FIGURE 23-3 [Ctrl] and cursor keys

The Function Keys

These are also largely the same as in Write, although there is, of course, a different set of commands on **[F2]**. We shall get back to those in the next section, but first, let's pick up the minor changes in the **[F]** keys.

[F3] – *Goto*
This is a real boon with big spreadsheets, for it offers two ways of jumping to a specific field.

72

The sheet and the screen

Goto field will move the cursor to the field identified either by its name or its co-ordinate address.

Goto search allows you to find a field on the basis of its contents.

At the 'enter :' prompt, type in the data that you are looking for. If you make a mistake, use the **[F4]** key to switch into edit mode.

As with the search routine in Write, you can hunt forwards or backwards. But there are other possibilities here. You can limit the search to the current row or column, or search the whole sheet with the 'both' option. Point to **row**, **column** or **both** and press **[Enter]** to set the search pattern, then select either **next** or **previous**.

```
Searching for VAT in both rows and columns
[Next] Previous Row Column Both
Search for the next occurrence          F1 — Help; Esc — Continue
```

[F4] – *Edit Field*

The main differences to note here are in the **width** routine. In Write, you could alter the width of an individual field by stretching or shrinking it with the arrow keys. In Spreadsheet, any changes of width apply to all the fields in the same column – that is inevitable with the grid structure – and the re-sizing is managed in another way. You can use the **set** option to specify the number of characters, or the **increase-by-1** and **decrease-by-1** options to make minor adjustments.

[F5] – *Pick Up*

You can **pick up** a single field without having to shade it first. Its contents can then be copied into another field by pressing **[F6]**. Do note that it is only the *results* of calculations, and not the formulae, that are copied by this method. The commands, **copy** and **move**, offer two alternative methods of transferring data within the sheet.

If you want to **pick up** more than one field, then you must use **[F7]** first to **shade** the block.

Copy Move Blank Titles ·Insert Remove Print

If you are keen to start creating some working spreadsheets, you might like to skip this section, and refer back to it later at need. If you prefer to know what everything does before you start to do anything serious, read on.

Some of these commands can only be used with shaded blocks; others may be used with single fields or with blocks. Where a block is needed, press [F7], highlight the block then, while you are still within the **shade** routine, press [F2] to call up the command menu.

Copy

This can be used for making single or multiple copies of a single field or a block, and can prove to be a valuable time-saver when constructing a sheet. When a formula is copied to another part of the sheet, any field co-ordinates are automatically adjusted to fit the new position. This means that where you need a set of formulae that are all basically the same – for example, totalling calculations at the end of every row in a block – you only need to write the first. This can then be copied across all the rest.

Note that the copied block will overwrite any existing cell contents, so do make sure that there is room for the copies.

One-to-One Copying

If a block is to be copied, **shade** it before you call up **copy**. When asked for the 'destination', point to the top left corner of the place that the new block will occupy.

One-to-Many Copying (Single Fields)

To mark off the 'destination' area for the copies, move the cursor to a corner of the area, press [F7] then fix that corner by pressing [.]. Move the cursor again to the opposite corner, to highlight the block, then press [Enter] to complete the command.

■ SECTION 24
The Spreadsheet commands

You can make multiple copies of a **single field**. The destination may be a single row or column , or a rectangular block.

```
    A       |   B    |   C    |   D    |   E    |   F      |
 1 Sales
 2            Spring   Summer   Autumn   Winter   Total
 3 North      10,000   15,000   12,000   10,000   +TOTAL(B3..E3)
 4 South      15,000   20,000   15,000   12,000   +TOTAL(B4..E4)
 5 East        8,000   10,000   10,000    8,000   +TOTAL(B5..E5)
 6 West        7,000    9,000   10,000    8,000   +TOTAL(B6..E6)
 7
 8 Totals     +TOTAL(B3..B6)
 9
10
```

FIGURE 24-1 Copy in use

Figure 24.1 shows a simple sales summary spreadsheet in the course of construction. For clarity, the annual totals, in column F, are given as formulae rather than as results. The formula +**TOTAL(B3..E3)** was written into field F3. When this was copied into the row, F4..F6, the row numbers in the formulae were altered to suit the position. To complete the table, the spreadsheet's creator would go through these steps:

1 place the cursor on B8;

2 press **[F2]** and select the Copy command;

3 Shade C8 to F8;

4 press **[Enter]** to complete the command.

■ SECTION 24
The Spreadsheet commands

One-to-Many Copying (Shaded Areas)

This is possible with single rows and columns only. You cannot create multiple copies of a rectangular block. Quite apart from anything else, it would be next to impossible to define the destination area!

A typical use of this version of the command is shown in Figure 24.2. There, each column will contain the figures and the calculations for a month. To copy column B across the rest of the year, you would need this sequence of operations:

1   press **[F7]** and shade B5 to B13;

2   press **[F2]** and select Copy;

3   move the cursor to C5;

4   press **[F7]** then **[.]** to fix C5 as a corner;

5   spread the shading across to cover the row C5 to M5;

6   press **[Enter]** to complete the command.

```
        A    |    B     |     C     |    D    |     E     |    F
1            | January  | February  | March   | April     | May
2    Sales A
3    Sales B
4
5    Total Sales   +B2 +B3
6
7    Purchases
8    Gross Profit  +B5 −B7              •
9
10   Expenses
11   Wages
12
13   Net Profit    +B8 −B10 −B11
```

FIGURE 24-2 Copying a block of cells

The Spreadsheet commands

Move

Use this, when reorganising a sheet, to move a single field or a shaded block from one part of the sheet to another. The moved block will overwrite any existing field contents at the new position, and its previous site will be left blank.

Move is quite different from **copy** in its treatment of formulae. If there are any in the block, only their results will be moved. The formulae themselves will be lost. So, if you want to keep the formulae when you move a block, use the **copy** command instead, then clear the old block by blanking.

Blank

This will wipe clear a single field or shaded block. Any references to blanked fields in other parts of the sheet will then show an error report.

Titles

When a spreadsheet expands beyond the confines of a single screen, it can become difficult to tell where you are in relation to row and column headings. This command allows you to fix the top row(s) and left hand column(s) of the sheet as titles. Then, when the sheet is scrolled, the headings will remain visible.

The Spreadsheet commands

	A	G	H	I	J	K	L	M
1	Cuddles '88							
2								
3		June	June	Aug	Sept	Oct	Nov	Dec
4								
5	Soft Toys	5000	7000	12000	15000	18000	14000	10000
6	Knitwear	1000	2000	5000	6000	8000	6000	4000
7	Beachwear	2500	1000	500	0	0	0	0
8	Total Sales	8500	10000	17500	21000	26000	20000	14000
9								
10	Materials	3825	4500	7875	9450	11700	9000	6300
11								
12	Gross Profit	4675	5500	9625	11550	14300	11000	7700
13								
14	Overheads	7040	5400	7200	10040	9240	7800	8360
15								
16	Net Profit	-2365	100	2425	1510	5060	3200	-660
17								
18	Balance	-3465	-3365	-940	570	5630	8830	8170
19								
20								

Spreadsheet: TITLEDEM   26% Free

Enter M2:

F1 - Help	F3 - Goto	F5 - Pick Up	F7 - Shade	F9 - Flip
F2 - Commands	F4 - Edit Field	F6 - Put Down	F8 - Calc/Draw	F10 - Done

FIGURE 24-3 Column A fixed with titles

■ **SECTION 24**
The Spreadsheet commands

Whether you fix the top rows or the left columns or both as titles, depends upon the position of the cursor when the command is given. Rows above and columns to the left of the cursor become titles. On a spreadsheet such as the one in Figure 24.4:

> with the cursor in A2, only the month headings will be fixed; scroll the screen to the right, and the headings in column A will disappear;

> with the cursor in B1, only the category headings will be fixed, and the month names will be lost when the sheet is scrolled up;

> with the cursor in B2, both left and top headings become fixed.

```
      A          B          C         D          E          F
 1          January    February   March     April      May
 2  Sales A      5000       6000      6500       7000       6500
 3  Sales B      3000       4000      3000       3500       4000
 4
 5  Total Sales +B2+B3    +C2+C3    +D2+D3     +E2+E3     +F2+F3
 6
 7  Stock Costs  4500       5500      5000       6000       5500
 8  Gross Profit +B5−B7    +C5−C7    +D5−D7     +E5−E7     +F5−F7
 9  Expenses     1500       1200      1600       1500       2000
10  Net Profit  +B8−B9    +C8−C9    +D8−D9     +E8−E9     +F8−F9
```

FIGURE 24-4 Using titles

Insert

It is all too easy, when designing a sheet, to forget some significant item; and even a well-structured sheet may need to be expanded or reorganised after it has been in use for a while. When that happens, you can always fit extra rows or columns into the sheet with this command.

Before you call up **insert**, place the cursor at the point on the sheet where the extra space is needed. If you are inserting rows, the row containing the cursor (and all beneath it) will be moved down. When columns are inserted, the one containing the cursor (and all to its right) will be moved to the right.

You will be offered the choice of **rows** or **columns**, then prompted for the number of lines to insert. Enter the number to complete the command.

The Spreadsheet commands

Field references in formulae will be adjusted as necessary to suit the new structure of the sheet. Figure 24.5 shows part of the sales sheet before and after inserting 1 Row, with the cursor on A10.

```
     A    |    B    |    C    |    D    |    E    |    F
 1│      January  February  March    April    May
 2│ Sales A    5000      6000      6500      7000      6500
...
 9│ Gross Profit +B5-B7    +C5-C7    +D5-D7    +E5-E7    +F5-F7
10│ Expenses     1500      1200      1600      1500      2000
11│ Net Profit  +B8-B9    +C8-C9    +D8-D9    +E8-E9    +F8-F9
```

```
     A    |    B    |    C    |    D    |    E    |    F
 1│      January  February  March    April    May
 2│ Sales A    5000      6000      6500      7000      6500
...
 9│ Gross Profit +B5-B7    +C5-C7    +D5-D7    +E5-E7    +F5-F7
10│
11│ Expenses     1500      1200      1600      1500      2000
12│ Net Profit  +B8-B10   +C8-C10   +D8-D10   +E8-E10   +F8-F10
```

FIGURE 24-5 Inserting a row

Remove

Use this to cut unwanted rows or columns from the sheet. Although the direct opposite of **Insert**, its routine is managed in quite a different way. In the example in Figure 24.6, a re-organisation in the sales department has meant that there is no purpose in having separate categories of sales. The top three rows can therefore be removed, and in future, the total figures will be written in directly. Here is how it is done.

1 Place the cursor in A2 – in practice any field in row 2 will do.

2 Press **[F7]** – Shade, and spread the highlight area down to A4. Though only the fields A2, A3 and A4 are actually shaded, rows 2, 3 and 4 are thus marked for removal.

3 Press **[F2]**, select Remove, then Rows and confirm that the Shaded rows are to be removed.

4 After this particular removal operation, all of the formulae will display error messages, because they all ultimately depend upon the existence of the sales figures. However, as soon as the 'Total Sales' formulae are replaced by values, the other formulae will perform properly again.

	A	B	C	D	E	F
1		January	February	March	April	May
2	[Sales A]	5000	6000	6500	7000	6500
3	[Sales B]	3000	4000	3000	3500	4000
4	[ ]					
5	Total Sales	+B2+B3	+C2+C3	+D2+D3	+E2+E3	+F2+F3
6						
7	Stock Costs	4500	5500	5000	6000	5500
8	Gross Profit	+B5−B7	+C5−C7	+D5−D7	+E5−E7	+F5−F7
9						
10	Expenses	1500	1200	1600	1500	2000
11	Net Profit	+B8−B10	+C8−C10	+D8−D10	+E8−E10	+F8−F10

FIGURE 24-6 Removing a row

Print

The Spreadsheet **print** command is identical to the Write version, with one exception. The alternative to printing all the spreadsheet is to print only a shaded part of it. If you want to do this, shade the area first, before calling up the Print command, then select **shaded** from the **range** option.

If the area to be printed is too wide, it will be printed in strips, each containing as many full columns as possible, and extending for the full depth of the sheet. Sideways printing, and the use of the slimmer typefaces offer alternative ways of coping with wide sheets.

The Other Spreadsheet commands

Data-fill Sort Transpose Lock Recalc Values Consolidate File Quit

Data-fill

This intriguing little utility will fill a shaded area with a sequence of numbers. The sequence may start at any value and increase or decrease by any regular step. Rows are filled left to right, columns top to bottom, and rectangular blocks are filled row by row from the top.

In Figure 25.1, three areas were shaded and Data-filled.

```
A1..A10      Start Value 1  Step Size 1
B1..F1       Start Value 20 Step size −5
C5..E8       Start Value 10 Step Size 10
```

	A	B	C	D	E	F
1	1	20	15	10	5	0
2	2					
3	3					
4	4					
5	5		10	20	30	
6	6		40	50	60	
7	7		70	80	90	
8	8		100	110	120	
9	9					
10	10					

FIGURE 25-1 Data-fill in use

The command can be useful where lists of reference numbers are needed, or where you want a quick set of values to test out a function.

The Other Spreadsheet commands

Sort

Where a spreadsheet is being used to store data, this command can be used not just for organising the data, but also for bringing aspects of it to the fore. In the example in Figure 25.2, the sheet is being used for keeping track of debts.

```
       A            |      B         |      C        |     D      |
 1 | Customer       | Ref. Num.      | Amount Owing  |
 2 | Jackson        | JY12/045       |       750.00  |
 3 | Smith          | SP05/121       |     1,000.00  |
 4 | Allens         | MR21/093       |       400.00  |
 5 | Dodson         | JU19/104       |     1,500.00  |
 6 | Brown          | AP05/049       |     2,000.00  |
 7 |
```

FIGURE 25-2 Sort – before

The customers' records can be entered as they come to hand, then sorted into alphabetical order afterwards. That would be done by the following sequence:

1 **Shade** the area containing the data – from A2 to C6.

2 Call up the **sort** command and ask for a sort on column A.

3 Select **ascending** Order.

The Other Spreadsheet commands

The sorted sheet is shown in Figure 25.3. When the firm's credit controller wants to find those customers that owe the most, the **sort** command can be used again. This time the area would be sorted on the basis of the data in column C, and a **descending** order sort would be used. This would bring those cutomers with the biggest debts to the top of the list.

	A	B	C	D
1	Customer	Ref. Num.	Amount Owing	
2	Allens	MR21/093	400.00	
3	Brown	AP05/049	2,000.00	
4	Dodson	JU19/104	1,500.00	
5	Jackson	JY12/045	750.00	
6	Smith	SP05/121	1,000.00	
7				

FIGURE 25-3 After the sort

Generally speaking, formulae are unaffected by the sort – that is to say, any field references will be adjusted to suit the new order. Thus, if C7 held the formula '+TOTAL(C2..C6)', it would still be the same after sorting, even though the contents of C2 and C6 have been moved. Difficulties might arise if C7 was included within the area to be sorted. Then its range references could become confused.

Transpose

This may be useful when restructuring a sheet, although it has a significant limitation. With it, you can swing a rectangular block of fields through 90 degrees, from lengthwise to widthwise or *vice versa*. The limitation is that it cannot be used if the block holds any kind of formulae or field references. Its main use is probably in swinging a set of headings over from rows to columns in the early stages of building a sheet.

Lock

This can give some measure of security to data and formulae. As the protection can easily be removed, it will not stop deliberate tampering but will prevent the accidental overwriting of a field.

■ SECTION 25
The Other Spreadsheet commands

Shade the area containing the fields you want to protect – that may even cover the whole spreadsheet – then call up **lock** from the **other** commands. You will be offered the choice:

All Non-formula Formula

Where the spreadsheet is to be reused with different sets of data, select **formula** only. The **non-formula** option is useful for locking headings. **All** refers to all types of fields within the shaded area, not all the sheet.

In the last stage of the command routine, the line menu offers:

Lock Unlock

Use this to turn protection on or off. Once a field has been locked, you can only edit or rewrite its contents by unlocking it first.

Recalc

In its default mode, all the formuale in the spreadsheet are recalculated every time any alteration is made to the sheet. This takes very little time, but it can be enough to slow things down if you want to enter a lot of data. At these times, you should call up the **recalc** command and turn automatic recalculation off before you start. When you need to get some results from the sheet, either press **[F8]** to get a single recalculation, or call up **recalc** and turn the automatic option back on.

A second aspect of this command concerns circular formulae. Sometimes you will have a spreadsheet where two or more formulae each depend upon the result of the other. The classic example is the Managing Director's bonus. This might be set at 10 percent of the final profit, but the final profit will depend upon the amount paid to the MD as a bonus.

SECTION 25
The Other Spreadsheet commands

```
        A         |      B       |       C    |      D      |
1 | Net Profit          99,000.00
2 | Bonus              +B3 * 0.10     +B2
3 | Final Profit       +B1 − B2
4 |
```

FIGURE 25-4 The MD's bonus

Type in this example (Figure 25.4) and you will see the <**CIRC**> message appear in B2. The spreadsheet recognises that the formula needs a value – from B3 – that will be calculated later. It will attempt the calculation, but displays <CIRC> to warn you that the result is not to be relied upon. Because of the <CIRC> message, the only way to see the calculated value is to copy it into another field – hence the '+B2' formula in C2.

If you recalculate the sheet enough times – half a dozen will usually do the trick – an accurate result will eventually emerge. This then, is where the **many** option comes in.

Recalculations	Bonus	Final Profit
1	0	99,000
2	9,900	89,100
3	8,910	90,090
4	9,009	89,991
5	8,999.1	90,000.90

The alternative way to deal with circular calculations is to set up a check field where the result will be zero when the calculations have been worked through to a final answer. Then the **until zero** option can be used. A little care is needed here because of the way that the spreadsheet handles numbers. It works in binary arithmetic, while the numbers written into the sheet will always be ordinary decimals. In the conversion from decimal to binary and back there is a very small loss of accuracy. The net result is that where a field should contain zero, it may well have 0.00000001 or similar. Overcome this problem by using the **round** function to trim off the excess decimal places.

The Other Spreadsheet commands

Values

Where a field contains a formula, it will normally show the value that results from the calculation. Use this command to turn on the formulae display if they are needed for checking purposes. It is often worth following this up with a **print** command, as a large sheet can be examined more conveniently on paper than on the screen.

Consolidate

Suppose you have a set of sheets, all identical in structure, with each one containing the figures for a different month. At the end of the year, you need to total all those figures. The **consolidate** command gives you an easy way of doing this. It allows you to merge two sheets on top of each other with the contents of each pair of fields being added together. (They can also be subtracted, multiplied or divided, although in practice these options would rarely be used.) Note that *all* formuale are lost in this process – it is their values which are used.

You can only consolidate two sheets in any one operation, and both must be loaded from disk. So, where there are more than two, save the resulting sheet, then consolidate it with the next. Continue to save and consolidate until all the relevant sheets have been added into one.

File

This command is identical to the version in Write, and allows you to save the current spreadsheet, or load in a new one without leaving the spreadsheet system.

Quit

As in Write, this offers a way out of the spreadsheet system without saving the current file.

■ SECTION 26
Building a spreadsheet

The first task in creating any spreadsheet is to define exactly what you want it to do. Next, draft out your design on paper. This applies to even the simplest models. Skimp on the planning, and you will inevitably spend far more time afterwards correcting and rebuilding the sheet.

Plan the Sheet

The first example is of a spreadsheet to be used for writing invoices. It involves no complex formulae, and demonstrates a number of the key functions and features of the system. Its design will follow that of the normal pre-printed invoices:

```
Heading    —   firm's name
           —   customer's name
           —   date and invoice/ reference numbers

Working Area
     For each item
           — details, unit price and quantity
           — total price to be calculated (unit price * quantity)
           — room for eight items
     Totals for all items
           — less discount (variable, must be keyed in)
           — plus VAT (variable — key in)
           — VAT calculated on discounted total

Comment area — terms of trade
```

Layout

Now to turn this into a spreadsheet. We will start by getting the main layout organised. From the plan, we can see that the sheet will only need to be four columns wide. Column A can be set to 20 or 30 characters, to give lots of room for descriptions:

Place the cursor somewhere in column A, press **[F4]** – edit field, select width then use the set option and give the value 20.

10 or 12 characters will be sufficient for each of the others. We can set the widths of all three at once by using **[F7]** to shade a set of fields from column B to D. Then use edit field, width and set as before.

■ SECTION 26
Building a spreadsheet

Headings

The firm's name and address can now be typed into the top of the sheet. It can be placed wherever you like, and it does not matter if any text is longer than the width of its field. It will be allowed to spread across into the next field, as long as this is empty.

In the field next to the date heading, use the +**TODAY()** function, so that the date will be produced automatically. (You may remember meeting this in Section 19.) While the cursor is still on that field, call up **edit field** and **format**. Select **date** from the format menu, and choose whichever date display you prefer.

```
            A          |    B    |    C    |     D     |
 1 | (Firm's name)
 2 | (address line 1)
 3 | (address line 2)
 4 |
 5 | Invoice to:              Date        +TODAY()
 6 | (Customer's name)        Invoice No. (or ref)
 7 | (address line 1)
 8 | (address line2)
 9 |
10 |
11 | Details           Price      Quantity   Amount
12 | (item descriptions) (unit price) (no. sold)  +B12 * C12
13 |                                              +B13 * C13
14 |                                              +B14 * C14
15 |                                              +B15 * C15
16 |                                              +B16 * C16
17 |                                              +B17 * C17
18 |                                              +B18 * C18
19 |                                              +B19 * C19
20 |                                             ─────────────
21 |                               Sub-total+TOTAL(D12..D19)
22 |           Discount at              10%   +D21 * C22
23 |                                             ─────────────
24 |                               Total        +D21 — D22
25 |           VAT at                   15%   +D24 * C25
26 |                                             ─────────────
27 |                               Amount Due   +D24 + D25
28 |
29 | Terms:............
```

FIGURE 26-1 The invoice blank

After the item headings have been done, the next job is to write in the formulae, and it will help if you put in a few test figures, so that the formulae have something to work on. Type in '**5.00**' as the price of the first item, and '**2**' under the quantity heading. The formula to calculate the total for each line is 'Unit Price * Quantity', and on the layout used in Figure 26.1, that translates to the field references '+B12 * C12'.

Write or Point

You can get field references into a formula either by simply typing them in, or by *pointing*. As soon as you touch a cursor movement key, the co-ordinates of the current field will pop up into the data entry line. Move the cursor until it reaches the relevant field, then type in the next part of the formula, or press **[Enter]** to finish. For the formula '+B12 * C12', the sequence would be:

Move to D12, where the formula is to be written;
Type '+' to indicate a formula   **D12** = +
Move the cursor to B12   **D12** = +**B12**
Type '*'   **D12** = +**B12** *
Move the cursor to C12   **D12** = +**B12** * **C12**
Press **[Enter]**

Check that the result is what you would expect from your test numbers, and, if all is well, the formula can be copied down to work out the totals for the other item lines.

Put the cursor on D12
Press **[F2]** and select copy
Move to D13 and press **[F7]** – shade
Spread the highlight down to D19 and press **[Enter]**

As the formula is copied down, the field references will be adjusted so that they always refer to the B and C fields in the same row. You will find that the error message <**N/A**> (not applicable) shows up in all those fields where there is no data for the formulae to work on. Type in some more test data in other lines to check that the formulae are doing their job.

Building a spreadsheet

Lists and Ranges

To total up all the items in D21, we could write the formula '+D12 + D13 + D14 + D15....'. But there is a better way, and that is to use the **TOTAL** function, which will add up all the values in a set of fields. This can be defined either as a list or a range.

A *list* is a set of field co-ordinates, separated by commas. It would be used where the fields are scattered about the sheet. The list of fields can be written directly into the formula, e.g.:

+TOTAL(B4,C5,D12,B16)

Where the same list will be used in several formulae, it is more efficient to name the list, and to write the name and definition into the sheet. If you wanted to link the fields A4, A7 and B8 into a list called 'set1', you could do it by moving the cursor to a field away from the working area, say A40, then keying in **'set1=(A4,A7,B8)'**. A40 will then display [set1]. Whenever that name is used, the spreadsheet will look up the list in A40.

A *range* is a solid block of fields defined by the co-ordinates of any two opposite corners. In this case, the fields are together in a single row, so a range can be used in the formula:

+TOTAL(D12..D19)

The field references for the range can be typed in, or produced by pointing. To do this, move the cursor to the first cell, press **[.]** twice – if you do not type two dots, it will not work – and move down to the opposite end, shading the block. End by typing the closing bracket.

As with lists, the range can be named and defined in another field:

Enter A41: set2=(D12..D19)

That name can then be used in formulae, so that **+TOTAL(set2)** would produce the same result as **+TOTAL(D12..D19)**. It is often worth taking the trouble to define a name. They are far easier to remember than field co-ordinates; the name always refers to the same fields, even though their co-ordinates may be changed by a restructuring of the sheet; and named fields can be accessed from another file.

Finishing Touches

To finish the sheet, type in the simple arithmetical formula shown in Figure 26.1 and some test values for the discount and VAT. These should both be given as decimal fractions – 0.10 for 10%, 0.15 for 15%.

Columns B and D should now be formatted to give a money display. Shade the relevant parts of the columns first, before calling up edit field. Note that when setting the money format, you will be taken through a series of options. One of these will ask whether or not you want a leading $ sign. If you choose to have one, it may not be displayed on the screen, but will appear when the sheet is printed. The discount and VAT fields, C22 and C25, should be formatted as percentages for ease of reading.

Save the Sheet

When you are satisfied with the sheet, erase your test data from it, and save it under the name 'INVOICE'. Next time you need to create an invoice, load it back in, type in the details of the customer and the sale, and print it out. If you want to retain a copy of the invoice on disk, save it under a new name – pehaps the invoice reference number.

■ SECTION 26

Building a spreadsheet

An example of this spreadsheet in use is shown in Figure 26.2.

```
       A                    |      B      |      C      |      D      |
 1 | Cuddles Manufacturing Corporation
 2 | Unit 9, Mendip Industrial Estate
 3 | Ambridge
 4 |
 5 | Invoice to:                          Date          24/04/88
 6 | HappyKids                            Invoice No.   HK19/231
 7 | 125 High Street
 8 | Little Hampton
 9 |
10 |
11 | Details                  Price       Quantity      Amount
12 | Large Blue Gribbles      £12.00           1          £12.00
13 | Small Pink Gribbles       £4.00           2           £8.00
14 | Medium Green Gribbles     £8.00           5          £40.00
15 | Tiny Green Gribbels       £2.00           5          £10.00
16 | Huge Black Quibbles      £20.00           2          £40.00
17 | Little Yellow Quibbles    £5.00          10          £50.00
18 | Soft Furry Quibbles      £10.00           2          £20.00
19 | Blue Suede Trobbles      £30.00           4         £120.00
20 |                                                     _____
21 |                                      Sub-total      £300.00
22 |                          Discount at       10%       £30.00
23 |                                                     _____
24 |                                      Total          £270.00
25 |                          VAT at            15%       £40.50
26 |                                                     _____
27 |                                      Amount Due     £310.50
28 |
29 | Terms:   28 Days Net
```

FIGURE 26-2 The invoice in use

■ SECTION 27
Cashflow analysis

Invoicing is a valid use of a spreadsheet, but one that only scratches at the surface of the capabilities of this powerful tool. If you really want to make your spreadsheet earn its keep, set it loose on some 'what if?' analyses, or get it to work through a series of calculations to cost up alternative scenarios. That's what we are going to do in these next two sections.

One of the most common uses of spreadsheets is for cashflow forecasts. They are relatively easy to set up, involve a number of calculations that would be tedious to do by hand, and provide invaluable information for a business. In essence, the sheet looks at the business over a number of months (or other periods), notes the anticipated income and expenditure and works out the running balance. It can therefore provide early warnings of overdrafts, but it can also show what will happen if the cashflows are rescheduled in any way.

In this simple example, a joiner is planning to set up a business selling and installing fitted kitchens. He knows that wages and other expenses will total a steady £2,500 a month; that the average profit on each job will be £500; that he and his small team can install a maximum of eight a month; and that it will take a few months to reach full capacity. When he does get there, the business will show a monthly profit of £1,500. The question is, how much of an overdraft is he going to need to tide him over until that time?

The plan is very straightforward:

> For every month –
>   Number of Jobs times
>   Gross Profit   (at 500 per job)
>   less Fixed Costs
> = Net Profit/Loss

Carry the Net figure over to the next month.

SECTION 27
Cashflow analysis

	A MONTH	B	C	D	E	F	G	H	I	J
1	MONTH		1	2	3	4	5	6	7	8	9
2										
3	Jobs	0	2	3	4	6	8	8	8	8
4	Gross Profit	0	1000	1500	2000	3000	4000	4000	4000	4000
5	Fixed Costs	2500	2500	2500	2500	2500	2500	2500	2500	2500
6	Net Profit	−2500	−1500	−1000	−500	500	1500	1500	1500	1500
7										
8	Balance	−2500	−4000	−5000	−5500	−5000	−3500	−2000	−500	1000

FIGURE 27-1 A simple cashflow

The spreadsheet that will help to answer this question is shown in Figure 27.1. To create your own version – extended to cover twelve months – follow these steps:

1 Write the headings into row 1 and column A. Use the **width** command to expand the column to 12 characters.

2 Shade the area B1 to M1, and use the **data-fill** command to write the month numbers for you.

3 Into B4, type the formula +**B3*500**, to find the gross profit.

4 Type **2500**, for the fixed costs, into B5; and +**B4-B5** into B6.

5 Shade the area B4 to B6, call up **copy**, and shade from C4 to M4 as the destination area. The three fields will then be copied across the full year.

6 Type +**B6** into B8, to get the first month's balance.

7 Type +**B8**+**C6** into C8, for the second balance. Copy this formula across the area D8 to M8.

Cashflow analysis

The Sheet in Use

The quality of the results produced by the sheet depends very largely on the quality of the data fed into it. The saying 'garbage in, garbage out' applies to spreadsheets just as it does to other types of computing. As this is a new business, it is impossible to forecast future trading on the basis of a track record, but what we can do here is make reasonable predictions of the most likely, and the best and worst possible futures.

Our entrepreneur estimates that it will take six months of steady growth to reach full capacity. Figure 27.1 shows this scenario. On this basis, he will need overdraft facilities for the first nine months, with a maximum of £5,500 by the end of month 4. In the worst possible future, (Figure 27.2) the number of jobs only increases by one a month and it will be a full year before he gets out of the red. (If the business grows any slower than this, he will give up well before the end of the year!)

	A	B	C	D	E	F	G	H	I	J
1	MONTH	1	2	3	4	5	6	7	8	9
2										
3	Jobs	0	1	2	3	4	5	6	7	8
4	Gross Profit	0	500	1000	1500	2000	2500	3000	3500	4000
5	Fixed Costs	2500	2500	2500	2500	2500	2500	2500	2500	2500
6	Net Profit	−2500	−2000	−1500	−1000	−500	0	500	1000	1500
7										
8	Balance	−2500	−4500	−6000	−7000	−7500	−7500	−7000	−6000	−4500

FIGURE 27-2 More of a cash trickle

A spreadsheet model of this simplicity may be useful for drafting the rough outlines of the cashflow, but it is not the sort of thing that could be taken to the bank manager as part of a business plan. For that you would need to include at least the major complexities of the real world.

For a start, the 'fixed costs' will not actually be the same every month. Some bills are paid quarterly, other annually; allowance needs to be made for the purchase of new tools and machinery; there may be economies of scale once the level of business reaches a certain point; advertising and promotional discounts can increase costs at the start; and, of course, there will be bank charges on that overdraft!

■ SECTION 28
Circular solutions

Not every spreadsheet will give a result immediately. Some will contain formulae with circular arguments, that is, where the value of one depends upon the result of another which itself depends upon the first. (See the **recalc** command in Section 25.) There is such a pair in this next sheet, which once again demonstrates the spreadsheet's ability to provide valuable management information by costing up alternative futures.

Let's start by outlining the situation. The management and workforce of Whizzo Electronics are negotiating the annual wage increase. The workers are looking for a substantial increase, but the management does not want to see a drop in their profits. The market could bear a small price rise, but the remainder of the rise in the wage bill must be met by improved productivity.

There are a number of factors in the equation, and they are linked in the following ways:

```
Formulae                                               Where Used

Unit Production Costs = Labour + Materials Costs        (B7, C7)
Variable Costs = Unit Cost * Number of Units           (B11, C11)
Total Costs = Variable + Fixed Costs                   (B13, C13)
Sales Income = Unit Price * Number of Units            (B16, C16)
Net Profit = Sales Income — Total Costs                (B18,C16)
```

■ SECTION 28
Circular solutions

As you can see in Figure 28.1, those formulae apply both before and after the wage increase. Additional formulae are then needed to assess the effects of the proposed increase.

```
        Formulae                                          Where Used

New Labour Cost = Old Cost + Percentage Increase     (C6)
New Sales Price = Old Price + Percentage Increase    (C15)
New Productivity = Raise if Net Profit lower         (B3)
```

	A	B	C	D
1	Wage Increase?	(percentage)		
2	Price Increase?	(percentage)		
3	Productivity Up	+IF(C18<B18,B3+0.1,B3-0.1)	+B3	
4				
5	Materials	(per unit)	+B5	
6	Labour	(per unit)	+B6*(1+B1)	
7	Unit Cost	+B5+B6	+C5+C6	
8				
9	Production	(no. of units)	+B9*(1+B3)	+C9
10				
11	Variable Costs	+B9*B7	+C9*C7	
12	Fixed Costs	(fixed costs)	+B12	
13	Total Costs	+B11+B12	+C11+C12	
14				
15	Unit Sale Price	(per unit)	+B15*B2	
16	Sales Income	+B9*B15	+C9*C15	
17				
18	Profit	+B16-B13	+C16-C13	

FIGURE 28-1 Brackets show where data is needed

It is that last formula which is the most complex one in the sheet. For a start, it involves a circular calculation — the net profit depends upon the production level, and that depends upon the change in productivity. So, the sheet must be recalculated **many** times (six or so will do), and the value in B3 must be copied into another field so that it can be read (C3).

The other aspect to that formula is that it uses a logical test. It compares the values in the two net profit fields, and if C18 is lower than B18, it adds 0.1 to the value held in B3; if C18 is higher, it will subtract 0.1 from B3. (Remember that the field holds two distinct things — the formula, and the value produced by the formula.)

SECTION 28
Circular solutions

The Sheet in Use

Figure 28.2 shows what happens when the sheet is put to work on a proposed 20 percent wage increase and 3 percent price rise. After half a dozen recalculations, it finds that an unrealistic 18 percent rise in productivity would be necessary to pay for the higher wages. The management might then suggest an increase of 7.5 percent, and in a matter of seconds the sheet will tell them that this will only need a 2 percent rise in productivity. Further proposals from either side can then be costed, until an affordable wage rise is found.

	A	B	C	D
1	Wage Increase?	20%		
2	Price Increase?	3%		
3	Productivity Up....	<CIRC>	18%	
4				
5	Materials	£40.00	£40.00	
6	Labour	£60.00	£72.00	
7	Unit Cost	£100.00	£112.00	
8				
9	Production	10,000	<CIRC>	11800
10				
11	Variable Costs	£1,000,000.00	£1,321,600.00	
12	Fixed Costs	£300,000.00	£300,000.00	
13	Total Costs	£1,300,000.00	£1,621,600.00	
14				
15	Unit Sale Price	£150.00	£154.50	
16	Sales Income	£1,500,00.00	£1,823,100.00	
17				
18	Profit	£200,00.00	£201,500.00	

FIGURE 28-2 The sheet in use

It is important to remember that this kind of sheet does not displace the manager as the decision-maker. But, by costing up the alternatives, it provides the information upon which meaningful decisions can be based. This was only a simple example and the calculations that were needed here could have been performed by hand without too much trouble. In a real-life situation, there would usually be more inter-linked factors and more calculations to perform. That is when the spreadsheet's ability to produce fast and accurate results makes it an invaluable aid to better management.

Mathematical Ability

These next three sections provide a survey of Ability's built-in calculating functions. Though they will be mainly used within spreadsheets, it is important to remember that almost all of them can be used anywhere within Ability.

Where a function requires a value, this can be written in directly, given as a field reference or name, or be the result of a calculation within the expression. For example:

```
+SQRT(81)
+LOG(B14)
+INT(sales_increase)
+ABS(C14–B12)
```

ABS(number)

This strips off the positive or negative sign, returning the absolute value of the number. It is particularly useful if you need to find the difference between two values, no matter which is the greater:

$$+ABS(9–6) = +ABS(6–9) = 3$$

EXP(power)

The inverse of **LN**, this exponential function raises *e* to the given power. Ability holds *e* to 12 decimal places:

$$+EXP(1) = 2.718281828459$$

INT(number)

This lops off the decimal fraction from a number, leaving only the integer.

$$+INT(2.3456) = 2$$

LN(number)

The inverse of **EXP**, this gives the natural logarithm of a number.

LOG(number)

This returns the base 10 logarithm of a number.

$$+LOG(1000) = 3 \quad \{ 10^3 = 1000 \}$$

Mathematical Ability

MOD(number,divisor)

The modulo of a number is the remainder from integer division. To find the other aspect of integer division – how many times a number can be divided by a second – use INT and the normal division sign. Thus:

+MOD(23,5) = 3
+INT(23/5) = 4

23 divided by 5 goes 4 remainder 3.

A possible use for modulo division would be in a coin and note analysis on a payroll spreadsheet. The section to deal with whole pounds is shown in figure 29.1. Pence would follow a similar pattern.

```
                    Formulae                    Results
     A       |      B      |      C      | | |   B   |   C
30 | Net Wage |       77.53
31 | Whole Pounds  +INT(B30)                      77
32 | 20_s         +INT(B31/20)  +MOD(B31,20)       3       17
33 | 10_s         +INT(C32/10)  +MOD(C32,10)       1        7
34 | 5_s          +INT(C33/5)                      1
35 | 1_s          +MOD(C33,5)                      2
```

FIGURE 29-1 Modulo division

RAND(number)

This will produce a random number in the range 0 to **number**. The number will have a long fractional part, and will generally need to be trimmed by **INT**, before it is much use. To simulate a die, giving numbers between 1 and 6, you would need:

+INT(RAND(6))+1

SECTION 29
Mathematical Ability

ROUND(number,decimal_places)

Ability holds numbers to 12 decimal places, which may give more accuracy than is either useful or desirable. The number of decimals included in the screen display can be set by the fixed format, but this does not change the actual value held by the spreadsheet. Use ROUND, where necessary, to trim the value down to a specific level of accuracy.

+ROUND(123.45678,3) = 123.457
+ROUND(0.00034,0) = 0

SQRT(number)

This calculates the square root of a number.

+SQRT(81) = 9

Combinations and Permutations

These next three functions may come in useful when you are working out how to fill in your football pools, or are involved in any other operation involving chance.

items refers to the total number of items;
set_size means the number in each group.

COMB(items,set_size)

In a combination the order in which items appear in a group is irrelevant. The sets {ABC}, {ACB}, {BAC}, {BCA}, {CAB} and {CAB} are all equivalent and count as only one combination. This function tells you how many combined groups of *set_size* can be produced from the given number of *items*. For example,

+COMB(4,2) = 6

four items can be combined into groups of two in six different ways. {ABCD} can produce the pairs {AB}, {AC}, {AD}, {BC}, {BD}, {CD}.

FACT(number)

The factorial of a number is that number multiplied by every integer down to 1. Factorial 4 = 4 * 3 * 2 * 1 = 24. It tells you the number of different ways in which the items in a set may be

102

SECTION 29
Mathematical Ability

ordered. Factorial 3 = 6, and the three letters A,B,C can be arranged as {ABC}, {ACB}, {BAC}, {BCA}, {CAB} and {CAB}. To put it another way, in a three-horse race, you have got a 1 in 6 chance of predicting the finish correctly.

Factorial numbers grow at an alarming rate, although Ability seems to manage them without too much bother. Factorials of large numbers take a little while to calculate, but it does not give up until you try to push it beyond factorial 720. That works out to 7.254 E 306 – that's 7.254 * 10^306 or 7,254,000 followed by 300 more 0's!!

```
+FACT(2)  =          2
+FACT(3)  =          6
+FACT(4)  =         24
+FACT(5)  =        120
+FACT(6)  =        720
+FACT(7)  =       5040
+FACT(8)  =      40320
+FACT(9)  =     362880
+FACT(10) =    3628800
```

PERM(items,set_size)

In a permutation, the order of items is important – {AB} and {BA} count as two different permutations. If this has echoes of the factorial function, it is because factorials are a key part of the equation that works out the number of possible permutations. In case you are interested, the equation is:

$$PERM(items,set\_size) = \frac{FACT(items)}{FACT(items - set\_size)}$$

The formula +PERM(4,2) gives the answer 12, because you can arrange any two items out of four in 12 different ways. From the set {ABCD}:

```
{AB}    {BA}    {CA}    {DA}
{AC}    {BC}    {CB}    {DB}
{AD}    {BD}    {CD}    {DC}
```

Mathematical Ability

Statistical Functions

All of these functions process the values in a set of fields. This may be a **list**, e.g., (A4,A6,A9,B7,B9), or a **range**, e.g., (B5..C15). Where a number of functions are to be performed on the same set, it may be more convenient to name the set, then use the name within the function.

The examples given below all use the values in the range A1..E1. With the expression 'sample=(A1..E1)' written into A2, the name 'sample' can be used within the functions.

```
     A    |    B    |    C    |    D    |    E    |
 1 |      1 |       3 |       4 |       5 |       7 |
 2 | [sample]
```

AVERAGE(set) or AVG(set)

This gives the mean or arithmetic average, found by adding together all the values and dividing by the number of values.

+AVG(sample) = 4   {20 / 5 = 4}

COUNT(set)

The number of values in the set. Any blank fields will be ignored, but those containing 0 or text will be included in the count.

+COUNT(sample) = 5

MAX(set)

The maximum value in the set.

+MAX(sample) = 7

MIN(set)

The minimum value in the set – ignoring blank cells.

+MIN(sample) = 1

■ SECTION 29
Mathematical Ability

STD(set)

The standard deviation is the most commonly used measure of the spread of values within a set. It is the square root of the Variance – see below. In practical terms, you would expect to find two-thirds of all values to fall within 1 standard deviation either side of the mean for the set. (For the figure to be of real use, the set must be of a reasonable size – at least 30 items.)

+STD(sample) = 2

SUM(set) or TOTAL(set)

These are alternative names for the same function. Both give the total of the values in the set.

+TOTAL(sample) = 20

VAR(set)

This calculates the variance of the items in the set. Variance is defined as the mean squared deviation of the items from the mean.

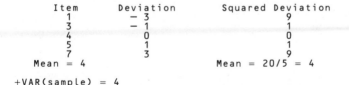

```
     Item        Deviation        Squared Deviation
      1            − 3                   9
      3            − 1                   1
      4              0                   0
      5              1                   1
      7              3                   9
  Mean = 4                     Mean = 20/5 = 4

+VAR(sample) = 4
```

WAVG(list1,list2)

The AVG function finds the average of a set of individual items, but often data has been collected into a frequency table. In these cases, use the Weighted AVeraGe function to find the mean. 'list1' will contain the values, 'list2' the number of items in each group.

■ SECTION 29
Mathematical Ability

Suppose a dress shop recorded the number of dresses of each size sold in a day, and wanted to know the average size. The data could be handled by a simple list:

8, 8, 10, 10, 10, 10, 12, 12, 12, 14

+AVG(list) = 10.6

Or it could be recorded into a frequency table:

```
Size           Number
  8              2
 10              4
 12              3
 14              1
```

+WAVG(size,number) = 10.6

The more items you have, the more sense it makes to use a frequency table and the WAVG function.

Trigonometry

Ability's trigonometrical functions all work in radians, not degrees. A *radian* is defined as that angle of a circle where the length of the arc is equal to the radius. There are, therefore, 2*PI radians in a full circle, and 1 radian is equal to 360/(2*PI) or 180/PI degrees.

Mathematical Ability

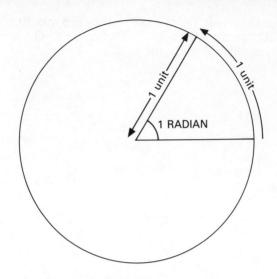

To convert between the two systems, use the formulae:

angle_in_degrees = angle_in_radians * 180 / PI()
angle_in_radians = angle_in_degrees * PI() / 180

PI()

Note the empty brackets. One of Ability's few rough edges is that it defines a function as something with brackets after its name. The fact that PI does not want anything after it is irrelevant. They must be there – and empty!

The constant is held to 12 decimal place accuracy.

+PI() = 3.141592653593

Mathematical Ability

The examples given below are all based on the right-angled triangle ABC, where AB=10cm, BC=5cm, AC=8.66cm, and angle A=30 degrees or 0.52 radians.

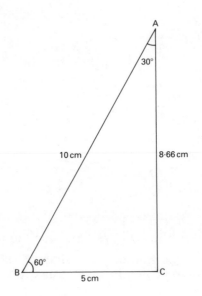

COS(angle)

The cosine of an angle, equivalent to the adjacent / hypotheneuse. The angle must be given in radians.

+COS(0.524) = 0.866

SIN(angle)

The sine of an angle, equivalent to the opposite / hypotheneuse.

+SIN(0.524) = 0.5

TAN(angle)

The tangent of an angle, equivalent to the opposite / adjacent.

+TAN(0.524) = 0.578

Mathematical Ability

ACOS(number)

The inverse of COS, the arcosine converts a cosine back into an angle, given in radians.

+ACOS(0.866) = 0.524 radians (30 degrees)

ASIN(number)

The arcsine, inverse of SIN.

+ASIN(0.5) = 0.524 radians (30 degrees)

ATAN(number)

The arctangent, inverse of TAN.

+ATAN(0.578) = 0.524 radians (30 degrees)

ATAN2(x,y)

This gives the bearing, from the origin, of a point defined by its x,y co-ordinates. In a right-angled triangle, the x,y values would be equivalent to the lengths of the adjacent and opposite sides.

+ATAN2(8.66,5) = 0.524 radians (30 degrees)

■ SECTION 30
Financial Ability

These functions all deal in various ways with the complexities of compound interest. Fortunately for us, all we need to know is what sort of values to stick in where. Ability can be safely left to cope with the rest.

In the examples given below, interest rates are all shown in percentages and on an annual basis. There are two points to note here.

You can write a percentage value into a field either as a percentage (followed by the % sign) or a decimal – 5% is the same as 0.05. Whichever you do, the value will be displayed as a decimal until you **format** the field as a percentage.

It makes no difference to the spreadsheet system if you work on an annual, monthly or daily basis. The important thing is that you must use the same time units for the interest rate and for the period of the loan. And do not forget that, with compound interest, the monthly rate is not simply one-twelfth of the annual rate. 1 percent per month works out at 12.68 percent per annum.

I make no apologies for always using 10 percent as the interest rate. It keeps the figures almost manageable.

Loans and Investments

PMT(capital,interest,periods)

This calculates the regular payments needed to repay a loan over a given number of periods – the most obvious example would be a mortage on a property.

	A	B	C
1	Capital	30,000.00	
2	Interest Rate	10%	
3	Term of Years	20	
4	Annual Repayment	3,523.79	+PMT(B1,B2,B3)
5	Monthly Repayment	293.65	+B4/12
6	Total Repayment	70,475.77	+B4*B3

COMPOUND(capital,rate,periods)

This calculates the final value of a lump sum invested at a fixed rate over a period of time, and includes both the original capital and the accumulated interest. The function assumes that the interest is added to the capital at the end of each period.

	A	B	C
1	Capital	10,000.00	
2	Interest Rate	10%	
3	Term of Years	5	
4	Final Value	16,105.01	+COMPOUND(B1,B2,B3)
5	Total Interest	6,105.01	+B4-B1

You can see how the function works if you calculate the interest year by year:

Capital	Interest @ 10%	End of Year Value
10,000	1,000	11,000
11,000	1,100	12,100
12,100	1,210	13,310
13,310	1,331	14,641
14,641	1,464.10	16,105.10
Total Interest	6,105.10	

FV(payment,rate,period)

This finds the accumulated future value of a regular saving. The function assumes that both payments in, and addition of interest to, the capital occurs at the end of each period.

	A	B	C
1	Regular Amount	1,000.00	
2	Interest Rate	10%	
3	Term of Years	5	
4	Future Value	6,105.10	+FV(B1,B2,B3)

Worked out in full, the figures are:

Year	Start of Year	Interest	End of Year Value
1	0	0	1,000
2	1,000	100	1,100
3	2,100	210	2,310
4	3,310	331	3,641
5	4,641	464.10	6,105.10

Financial Ability

Discounted Cash Flows

The theory behind discounted cash flows is that a pound in the pocket is worth more than a pound to come. The money that you have now could be invested and earn interest, or it could reduce borrowing and save interest charges. Thus, if the interest rate is 10 percent, £900 now is worth as much as £990 in a year's time.

When the functions are being used to assess the value of potential investments, the *discount rate* is the return that the firm expects on its capital. It need not necessarily be the same as normal bank interest rates.

+PV(income,discount rate,period)

This function forms a useful bridge between investments and discounted cashflows, as it is the inverse of the **PMT** function. It returns the value, at present prices, of a regular income over a period of time. It could therefore be used to calculate the size of mortgage that could be obtained for any given annual payment.

	A	B	C
1	Payment	3,523.79	
2	Discount Rate	10%	
3	Term of Years	20	
4	Present Value	30,000.00	+PV(B1,B2,B3)
5			
6	Payment	1,000.00	
7	Discount Rate	10%	
8	Term of Years	5	
9	Present Value	3,790.79	

The first example is a back-calculation of the mortgage that was used to illustrate the PMT function. The second, simpler one is worked out fully below. The *discount factor* is the discount rate raised to the power of the year number — it is the way in which compound interest is taken into account. The payment is divided by this factor to find its present value.

Year	Payment	Discount Factor	Discounted Value
1	1,000	1.1	909.09
2	1,000	1.21	826.45
3	1,000	1.331	751.31
4	1,000	1.4641	683.01
5	1,000	1.6105	620.83
		Total Value	3,790.79

■ SECTION 30
Financial Ability

NPV(interest,cashflow)

The present value function can only be used where the returns on an investment are the same in each period. Where the investment under consideration is a manufacturing project, it is more likely that the returns will be far from regular. Rather than 'returns', we should be talking about 'net cash flows' – the balance of incomings and outgoings on the project. In these cases, the Net Present Value function should be used instead. This discounts a cash flow given as a range of values.

In some accounting conventions, the initial investment is deducted from the discounted cash flow to give a final figure for the NPV of the project. If this is a positive value, the project is deemed to be profitable – provided that the future cash flow estimates and discount rate are realistic and reliable. It should be noted that Ability's NPV function does not deduct the intial outlay.

	A	B	C	
1	Discount Rate	10%		
2				
3	Cashflow	Year	Discounted	
4	−10,000.00	0	−10.000.00	
5	2,000.00	1	1,818.18	
6	2,000.00	2	1,652.89	
7	4,000.00	3	3,005.26	
8	4,000.00	4	2,732.05	
9	2,000.00	5	1,241.84	
10		Total Discounted	10,450.23	
11				
12	Net Present Value	10,450.23	+NPV(B1, A5..A9)	
13	less Outlay	450.23	+B12−B1	
14				
15	Internal Rate of Return			
16	Best guess	10%		
17	Calculated rate	11.6%	+IRR(B16,A4..A9)	

FIGURE 30-1 Using net present value

IRR(guess,cashflow)

This provides an alternative means of appraising a project. It calculates the internal rate of return of a cashflow – that is, the discount rate at which the net present value would be nil. If the IRR value is higher than the discount rate used by the firm, then the project will be profitable.

Financial Ability

For the function to work, you must give an estimated value for the discount rate. This does not need to be anything like accurate. The function will return the same value, no matter how wild your guess!

In the example in Figure 30.1, the 'year' and 'discounted' columns are for interest only. They have no purpose for either the NPV or the IRR functions.

■ SECTION 31
Logical, index and date functions

IF(test,value_if_true,value_if_false)

With this function you can build quite a sophisticated level of decision-making into a spreadsheet. It tests the contents of a field, or fields, and, on the basis of that test, it allocates one of the two alternative values. A simple use for IF would be to work out whether or not an invoice qualified for a discount.

```
     A          |     B        |   C        |
41| Sales Total      1,420.00
42
43| Discount              10%
44|                   142.00
45
46| Net Total        1,278.00
```

This formula in B43 sets the discount level at 10 percent if the sales total is more than £1,000, or 0 percent if less. (Note that a *value_if_false* figure must be given, even if it is only 0.)

$$B43 = +IF(B41>1000,10\%,0)$$

Logical Operators

These six logical operators may be used when comparing values:

```
   =         equal to
   >         greater than
   <         less than
   >=        greater than or equal to
   <=        less than or equal to
<> or ~=     not equal to
```

The tests may be written inside IF functions, or used on their own. If a field contained the expression:

(B41>1000)

then it would have a value of 1 if this were true, or 0 if false.

A further three logical operators may be useful in certain circumstances:

```
&         AND
|         OR
~         NOT
```

Logical, index and date functions

There will be times when alternatives are dependent upon more than one condition – the discount may only be given if the invoice total is above the limit AND if it is a cash sale; or it may be given if the total is over the limit OR it is a favoured customer. In these circumstances, **&** (AND) and | (OR), come into play.

    +IF(B41>500 & B41<1000, 5%, 0)

With the ampersand linking the two tests, the sales total (in B41) must be both more than 500 AND less than 1,000 for the 5 percent discount to be given.

    +IF(B41>=1000 | customer=1, 10 percent, 0)

Here the field **customer** is assumed to hold '1' if the invoice is for a favoured customer, and '0' for others. If it is a special customer, OR sales are at least £1,000, OR BOTH conditions are met, the discount of 10 percent will be given.

Coping with Multiple Tests

Now, what if both of these pairs of conditions apply, and the discount level may be 5 percent, 10 percent or 0 percent depending upon the total and the type of customer? There are essentially two ways of managing multiple IFs.

The simplest approach is to set up a series of separate IF functions and pick out the highest level of discount. The workings could well be tucked away at the bottom or side of the sheet:

```
        A              |       B          |      C         |
41|  Favoured?                       1      {B41 named as customer}
42|  Sales Total               750.00      {B42 named as sales}
43|
44|  5% level?          +IF(sales>500 & sales<1000, 5%,0)
45|  10% level?         +IF(sales>=1000 | customer = 1, 10%,0)
46|
47|  Discount given     +MAX(B44,B45)
48|
```

The second approach is to write IF functions within other IF functions – the resulting formulae can be somewhat difficult to read, so let's simplify the discounting arrangements! The following formula is for a firm that gives discounts of 10 percent for sales over £1,000, 5 percent for sales over £500, and does not believe in favouritism.

    +IF(sales>1000, 10%, IF(sales>500, 5%, 0))

If the total is over £1,000 then the 10 percent discount is given after the first test, and the rest of the formula is ignored. If it is less, then the spreadsheet goes on to check the lower limit.

You can have any number of IF functions within each other, as long as each is properly written and stands in place of a 'value_if_true' or 'value_if_false' of the previous IF. However, in practice they are exceedingly prone to error. It is very easy to omit a bracket or a comma somewhere along the line, and just as easy to get confused by multiple levels of logical testing.

ISERR(set)

This will check a field, or a set of fields, for the presence of an error report – <N/A>, <DIV 0>, <OVER>, <CIRC>, etc. The function returns a value of 1(true) if errors are found, and 0 (false) otherwise.

The Index Functions

These three functions work with tabular data and operate in similar ways. They can draw data from a table, or check a value against a table. The following sample will be used as we look at each function in detail.

```
       A          |        B          |      C        |
1 | Ref No.         Description
2 |           101 Furry Quibbles
3 |           103 Leather Quibbles
4 |           200 Green Gribbles
5 |           201 Red Gribbles
6 |           250 Large Blue Trobbles
7 |           251 Large Pink Gribbles
8 |
9 | Ref to find      .....
```

FIND(key_number,table_of_numbers)

This will look for a number in a table of numbers, and tell you its position in the list. This may be written horizontally or vertically, but, for the function to work, the table must be in numerical order from left to right or top to bottom.

In the example, if B9 held '250', the formula:

+FIND(B9, B1..B7)

would return the value 5, as 250 is the 5th number in the list.

Logical, index and date functions

If there is no number which matches, then FIND returns the position of the last number which was smaller than the input value. If the input is larger than any in the table, it therefore FINDs the last position. Thus, if 300 were entered in B9, the FIND value would be 6.

Oddly, if the input value is *smaller* than any in the table, the function returns a value one higher than the size of the list. An input value of 50 would give the result '7' in this case.

INDEX(position,table_of_data)

The data table used with this function may contain text, values or a mixture of both. It takes the **position** number, counts through the table and displays whatever it finds in the field at the given position. Using the example above, the formula:

+INDEX(3,B2..B7)

would return 'Green Gribbles'.

If the position number is larger than the table size, then **INDEX** returns the last item in the table.

Neither **FIND** nor **INDEX** have much application by themselves, as they are rather incomplete functions. You really need to combine the position-finding ability of **FIND** with the data extraction of **INDEX** – and you can do that:

+INDEX(FIND(B9,B2..B7))

This would take the input value, **FIND** its position in the reference number list, then look up the description. However, if you want to do that sort of thing, it is usually quicker and easier to use the **LOOKUP** function.

LOOKUP(key,index_table,data_table)

This is FIND and INDEX in one function. It looks up the key number in the index table and displays the value in the adjacent data table. These must be written either as two rows, index immediately above data; or as two columns, with the index to the left of the data table.

+LOOKUP(B9,A2..A7,B2..B7)

Enter 103 into B9, and the function displays 'Leather Quibbles'

When trying to match numbers with the index table, **LOOKUP** follows the same rules as **FIND**, except that if the number is smaller than any in the index, **LOOKUP** gives you the first item from the data table.

The only occasions in which the combination of **FIND** and **INDEX** would be used in preference to **LOOKUP**, would be where the index and data tables could not be fitted into the sheet side by side.

Date Functions

TODAY

This returns the number of days since January 1 1900. If you really want to see what the date is, select a readable **date format**. The *date_value*, as such, may be of use in calculating the number of days that have elapsed since another given date.

Like **PI()**, the function is complete in itself, but must have brackets written after it because Ability expects all functions to have them.

DATE(year,month,day)

This converts a date, given as three numbers, or as three field addresses, into a date_value. It could be formatted for tidy display, or used in a calculation.

```
        A          |     B      |    C    |    D    |
1 |               Year         Month        Day
2 | Date of Sale          88           2          28
3 | Today is       +TODAY()
4 | Age of Debt    +B3-DATE(B2,C2,D2)
```

Assume that TODAY is 18 April 1988. B3 would display the date value 32250. The formula in B4 would convert 28 February 1988 (88,2,28) into 32200 and subtract this from 32250 to show that the debt was 50 days old – and overdue!

■ SECTION 31
Logical, index and date functions

DAY(date_value)

This and the next three functions all work in much the same way, and can be used for breaking a date value (normally found by **TODAY**) into its component parts.

DAY extracts the day number:

+DAY(32250) = 18

MONTH(date_value)

MONTH extracts the month number:

+MONTH(32250) = 4

YEAR(date_value)

YEAR extracts the year number, and displays it as four figures:

+YEAR(32250) = 1988

WEEKDAY(date_value)

This works out the day of the week, counting Sunday as 1 and Saturday as 7. 18 April 1988 fell on a Monday:

+WEEKDAY(32250) = 2

You can combine this function with a LOOKUP table to bring the day's name onto the sheet.

```
      A           |        B          |      C        |
 1 | Day of the Week
 2 |            1    Sunday
 3 |            2    Monday
 4 |            3    Tuesday
 5 |            4    Wednesday
 6 |            5    Thursday
 7 |            6    Friday
 8 |            7    Saturday
 9 |
10 | Day number     +WEEKDAY(TODAY())
11 |                +LOOKUP(B10,A2..A8,B2..B8)
```

If today was 18 April 1988, B11 would display 'Monday'.

PART FOUR

Graphs

■ **SECTION 32**

Turn numbers into pictures

When you are preparing printed reports or presentation 'slide-shows', it is often a good idea to use graphs as well as, or in place of, tables of numbers. It is not just a matter of prettying up the appearance. Most people find it easier to grasp the real import of figures when they are displayed in graphic form. Long term trends and regional or seasonal variations are much clearer as lines or sequences of bars than as series of detailed numbers; and atypical results, that might be missed in tabular data, will stand out from the crowd when graphed.

Graph can produce four types of display – bar charts and stacked bar charts, line graphs and pie charts. Apart from the pie charts, which can only handle one set of data, they can graph up to seven sets of figures at a time. (In practice, this is more than enough. It is a mistake to try to cram too much information into any graph.) Titles may be added, although there are, unfortunately, no means of including legends to label the bars or lines. The graphs can be printed by a dot-matrix printer, either by themselves or as part of a Write document; or drawn in black or colour by a plotter.

The GRAPH Screen

The Graph display occupies the major part of the screen. Its appearance is very similar to that of any paper copy, both in terms of the shading patterns of bars and pie wedges, and of the typefaces that are used for the text.

The data area on the left-hand side shows which *series*, or sets of figures, are in use. When a set of data is to be defined or edited, it is selected by pointing in this area. Similarly, individual series and shaded groups may be picked out from here for special display treatment.

The bottom of the screen is much the same as elsewhere in the Ability system. All information is passed to the graph through the data entry line, and, as usual, you must press **[F4]** if you want to edit the series beneath the screen cursor.

In the function key reminders you will see that **[F3]** – goto and **[F5]** – pick up are not active in Graph, but then there is nowhere to go to and nothing much to pick up.

Turn numbers into pictures

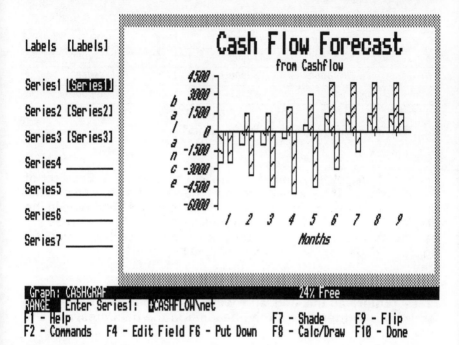

FIGURE 32-1 The Graph screen

The Bare Essentials

To produce a graph, all you really need are some figures. Everything else is optional. These figures can be drawn from a Spreadsheet, from fields in a Database or Write document, or be typed in directly. We will use this latter method in our first example.

Turn numbers into pictures

Software Sales 1987

	Spring	Summer	Autumn	Winter	
Mail Order	15,000	17,000	18,000	19,000	
Shops	14,000	8,000	12,000	16,000	
Export	9,000	9,000	11,000	10,000	

FIGURE 32-2 Information to be graphed

The numbers to be graphed are given in Figure 32.2. Each set of values, mail order, shops and export, needs to be entered as a list under one of the 'series' headings. Point to series1 and type in the first set at the prompt, as shown below. Notice that commas are used to separate the values – they must NOT be written inside the figures. '15,000' must be typed as '15000'.

Enter Series 1:15000,17000,18000,19000

Press **[Enter]** at the end and watch what happens. The label **[series1]** is written next to the heading in the data area, and the message:

Please wait: Drawing graph

appears at the bottom of the screen. After a moment you will see a bar chart, as in Figure 32.3.

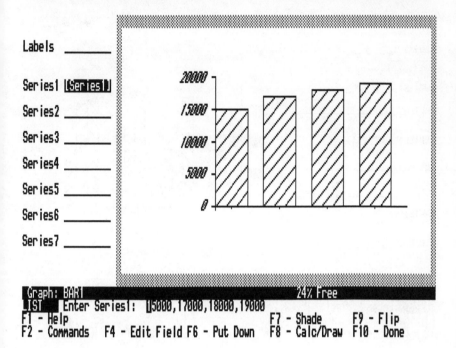

FIGURE 32-3 Series 1 graphed

Move the cursor to **series2** and type in the second set of figures. The chart will be redrawn, with two sets of narrower bars, side by side. Repeat the process with **series3**. All that is really needed now to complete the graph is to add some **labels**, so that you can see the relevance of each set of bars.

Move the cursor up to the top line and type in the headings at the prompt. As with the series, they should be entered as a list, separated by commas:

Enter Labels: Spring,Summer,Autumn,Winter

They will be added to the graph, and the first few characters of the list will appear next to the labels heading.

Turn numbers into pictures

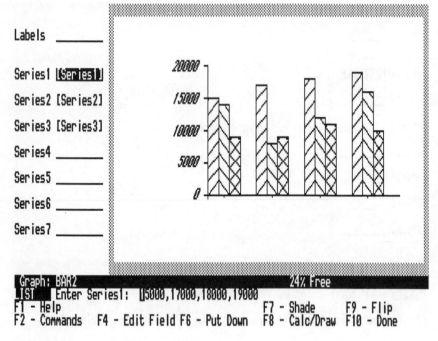

FIGURE 32-4 Ready for labels and titles

Editing

Should you have made a typing error, or wish to alter either the **labels** or the **series** data, move the screen cursor to the appropriate line and press **[F4]** – edit. The list will pop up in the data entry line and may be edited as normal. Press **[Esc]** or move the screen cursor when you have finished. Where major alterations are needed, it is usually quicker and easier to retype the whole list.

If all you want is simple bar charts that will help people to make sense of tables of numbers, then all you really need to know is how to key in the series and the labels. In the next section we will see how to get a more polished display, by using the command set. After that we will turn our attention to files and fields and find ways of bringing Spreadsheet data into graphs, and of including graphs within Write documents.

SECTION 33
The Graph commands

Style Design Titles Blank Hard-copy Redraw Others

Most of the commands and their options are self-explanatory. The main thing to realise is that some only apply to certain types of graph, and that to change the appearance of a series you must point at it, or include it in a shaded set.

When you press **[F2]** to call up the commands, Ability assumes that you will want to alter several of the graph settings. Therefore, as you finish with each option, it returns you to the command menu rather than going right back out to the data entry level.

Style

Notice that the **style** selection applies to the individual series, not to the graph as a whole – which you might have expected. So, if you are only pointing to one series when changing the style, the other series will continue to be displayed as they were before. This means that you can have lines and bars on the same chart – which may be useful sometimes. To change the style of the whole graph, use **[F7]** to shade all the series, before you call up the command menu.

■ SECTION 33
The Graph commands

Bar charts are probably the best choice for comparing sets of data. The relative sizes of adjacent bars give good set-to-set comparisons; and by focusing on one fill-pattern, you can see the variation within any one series. It is clear from Figure 33.1 that the mail order sales have been consistently better than either shop or export sales, and also that the shop sales fell dramatically during the summer and had not fully recovered by the end of the year.

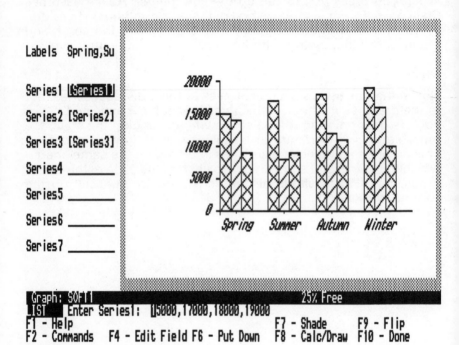

FIGURE 33-1 Bar charts

■ SECTION 33
The Graph commands

Stacked-bars are good for emphasising the cumulative effect of the different series, but tend to obscure the variation between and within them. This is particularly the case where you have a number of series. From Figure 33.2 we can see that overall sales have been improving steadily, apart from that dip in the summer, but it is hard to see how the export sales have performed over the year.

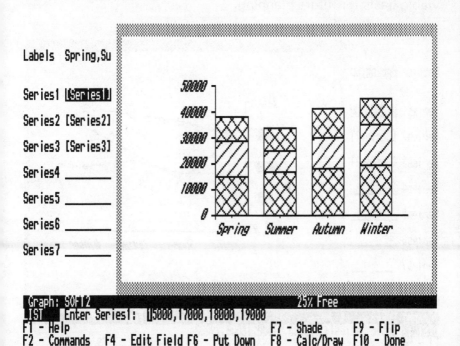

FIGURE 33-2 Stacked bars

SECTION 33
The Graph commands

Line graphs pick out trends, and lead the eye on to project into the future. From Figure 33.3, we might conjecture that shop sales will soon catch up with mail order sales, but that exports are on a slippery downward slope. In fact, it would be unrealistic to try to project from the limited data in this example. If the figures had been collected over a span of two or three years and the trend lines were reasonably smooth, then such projections could be a viable basis for future planning.

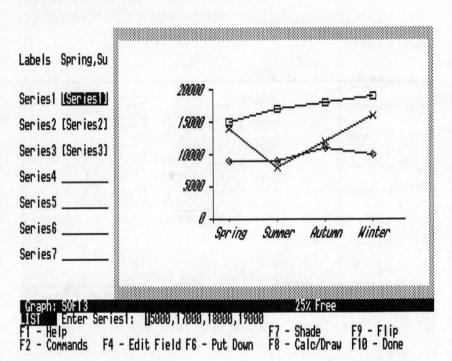

FIGURE 33-3 Line graphs

130

Pie charts can only be drawn where there is a single series. Their main purpose is to illustrate the contribution that each part makes to the whole; and to this end, the values in the series are converted to percentages and displayed by their wedges.

If you have keyed in all the software sales figures, you will have to remove two series with the **blank** command (see below) before you can change to a pie display. You may even prefer to blank the lot and start again with a new set of figures more suited to a pie format. (It might be an idea to try out some of the **design** options on the bar and line graphs before you do this.)

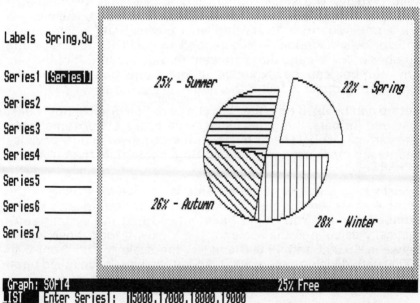

```
Labels  Spring,Su                   25% - Summer        22% - Spring

Series1 [Series1]

Series2 _____

Series3 _____

Series4 _____

Series5 _____

Series6 _____        26% - Autumn              28% - Winter

Series7 _____
```

```
Graph: SOFT4                                    25% Free
LIST    Enter Series1:  []5000,17000,18000,19000
F1 - Help                                     F7 - Shade    F9 - Flip
F2 - Commands    F4 - Edit Field F6 - Put Down  F8 - Calc/Draw F10 - Done
```

FIGURE 33-4 Pie charts

The Graph commands

Design

The sub-options to this command allow you considerable control over the final appearance of your graph. They are well worth exploring.

Fill-pattern can only work with bar and stacked-bar charts. Ability will automatically use a different pattern for each series, but you may not like the choice.

Point-marks are for line graphs only.

Explode wedge applies to pie charts, of course. Select **all** to 'explode' – pull out of the pie – all of the wedges; or **none** for a solid display. The **single** option acts as a toggle for individual slices, switching between exploded and unexploded. The wedges are numbered from 1, starting at 3 o'clock, and going round anticlockwise. Wedge 1 is exploded by default. Just type the number of the wedge that you want to move in or out of the pie. Any number can be exploded at the same time, though the highlighting effect is lost if this is overdone.

Rotate can be used on either bar charts or line graphs, but is best reserved for bars. It toggles between vertical and horizontal bars. The vertical display seems best for most purposes, if only because people are more used to scanning from left to right than from top to bottom.

Y-scale allows you to select **automatic** or **manual** scaling of the vertical scale, and to set the number of decimal places in the number display. You might have noticed that the system automatically calculated the scale for the Y-axis. It took those values between 15,000 and 19,000 and set the scale to run from 0 to 20000 with divisions every 5000. Ability can usually be relied upon to select a sensible scale, but this is not always the case.

■ SECTION 33
The Graph commands

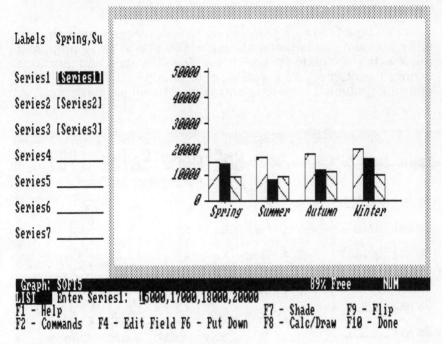

Labels Spring,Su

Series1 **[Series1]**

Series2 [Series2]

Series3 [Series3]

Series4 _____

Series5 _____

Series6 _____

Series7 _____

Graph: SOFT5   89% Free   NUM
LIST   Enter Series1: 15000,17000,18000,20000
F1 - Help   F7 - Shade   F9 - Flip
F2 - Commands   F4 - Edit Field F6 - Put Down F8 - Calc/Draw F10 - Done

FIGURE 33-5 The automatic scale fails!

Press **[Esc]** to leave the command menu, and edit series1 so that one of the values is 20,000. You should see that the automatic scaling routine does not do too well with this! (Figure 33.5) Where this kind of thing happens, use the manual option to tidy up the display. You will be prompted for the new maximum or minimum value — but notice that Ability graphs always start from 0. The *minimum* value only applies where you have negative numbers. It is not possible to set a scale to run from 10,000 to 20,000.

133

Titles

Text can be added to a graph in up to four places. The **main** title will be shown in a large typeface, the **sub-title** in small print, and the **X-axis** and **Y-axis** titles in italics. The size, style and positions cannot be altered, and if you want to change a title in any way, you must retype it — there is no means of editing titles.

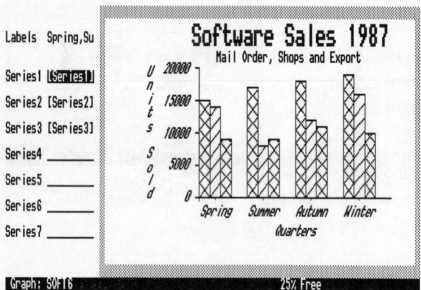

FIGURE 33-6 The finished graph

■ SECTION 33
The Graph commands

Blank

This is similar to the blank command in the spreadsheet. Use **[F7]** first to shade the series that you want to remove. To clear the whole graph, include the labels in the shaded area.

Hard-copy

Select **print** for output to a dot-matrix printer. None of the usual setting-up operations are required here, as there are only two ways that the graph can be printed. In the normal upright version, the graph is drawn rather small and sits by itself in the middle of a page; **sideways** produces very much larger graphs, almost filling an A4 sheet. (Note that upright and sideways refers to the whole graph; whether the bars have been rotated or not is another matter.

If you do not wish to print the graph immediately, use the **to-file** option to redirect the output to a file, in a printable form. Press **go** at the end, to send the graph to the disk or the printer.

The remaining options in this set apply only to plotters.

Quadrant selects the part of the paper on which the graph is to be drawn. It can be **full-page**, or quarter-size in any quadrant of the sheet. These are numbered as shown in Figure 33.7.

■ SECTION 33
The Graph commands

QUADRANTS

1st	2nd
3rd	4th

FIGURE 33-7 Plotter quadrants

Colors allows you to select the pen colour for different aspects of the graph – outline, fill patterns, axes, titles, X and Y labels and wedges. The method is always the same – just say which pen number to use. Use **wait** to hold the output while you change pens, if necessary.

When you have defined the plotter display, set the process in motion with **start plotting**.

Redraw

By default, the graph will be redrawn whenever you make any changes to it – just as a spreadsheet is normally recalculated constantly. If you want to type in a lot of data, or to run through the Commands setting display options, then redrawing can slow you down. In these cases, call up redraw and select **manual** control. After that, the graph will only be redrawn when you press **[F8]** – calc/draw.

■ SECTION 33
The Graph commands

Others – File & Quit

The **file** command is the same here as elsewhere. It allows you to save the graph or load a new one without leaving the graph part of the system.

Quit offers a way out of the system without saving the current graph.

PART FIVE

Integration

Files and fields

Ability offers a very high level of integration between the various parts of its system, and that is something that should never be forgotten. Data can be passed freely between named fields in different files. It does not matter whether they are Spreadsheets, Databases or Write documents; as long as the files are currently active (that is, you have been using them and they have not been 'Put-away') their data is available to the rest of the Ability system. Graph files are unusual in that you can only pass data into them and not out.

Earlier in the book you saw how the data in one field could be drawn into another, either as part of a formula or simply to transfer the value from one part of the spreadsheet or document to another:

+B3 − B5 + B7
10% * sales_total
+mortgage

Remember that if a field address or name is at the beginning of a formula, it is prefixed by a plus sign to show that it is a reference and not text.

It is almost as easy to draw data from fields in other files. The reference must include the filename, naturally; and you can only access fields that have been identified by name. Start with a plus sign, and separate the file name from the field name with a backslash:

+CASHFLOW\jan_balance

(Use capital or lower case letters at will. Ability will automatically convert the file name to capitals and the field name to lower case.)

■ SECTION 34
Files and fields

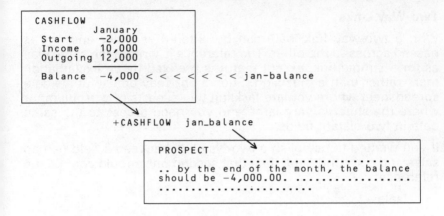

```
CASHFLOW
          January
   Start    -2,000
   Income   10,000
 Outgoing   12,000
          ────────
 Balance    -4,000  < < < <  < < <  jan-balance
```

```
        +CASHFLOW    jan_balance
```

```
PROSPECT
          ........................
  .. by the end of the month, the balance
  should be -4,000.00. .................
          ....................
```

That's all there is to it. The data that is transferred in this way is always up to date. Suppose this reference was written into the PROSPECT document – a lengthy letter to the bank explaining the anticipated cash flows. If an alteration is made to the CASHFLOW spreadsheet, so that the jan_balance field is revalued, that new value will be present in the document.

Data could be passed back from PROSPECT to CASHFLOW in the same way. Assume that the document contains a field named OVERDRAFT, in which is stored the overdraft limit set by the bank. To incorporate its value in CASHFLOW, you would write this reference into one of its fields.

　　+PROSPECT\overdraft

This type of link is one-way. Alter the jan_balance field in the CASHFLOW spreadsheet and the new value is passed to the PROSPECT document; but you cannot alter the jan_balance figure from the PROSPECT end of the same link. Should you want to do that, you would need to use two-way links.

Files and fields

Two-Way Links

With a two-way link, data can be entered at either end and is passed across to the other. The reference is written the same way as for a simple link, except that it is prefixed by an exclamation mark rather than a plus sign. Such a link may be useful inside a spreadsheet where you are tackling two aspects of a problem, or where the sheet is very large and you need access to the same data in two distant fields.

If you wanted to establish a two-way link between a field named **sales** and a second field, then that second one should contain the reference:

!sales

When you enter this, the second field will be given the same name as the one in the reference. In this case, both would take the name **!sales**.

It is exactly the same when linking between different files:

!INVOICE\discount

If that example had been written in a Write document, then afterwards the two fields would both be named **!discount**.

Two words of warning before we go any further:

■ If you try to write a two-way link in a named field, you will get an error message. The second field must be nameless at the start of the process.

■ The files from which you want to draw data must be active, either from recent use or currently in use in the other Flip state (see below). Even if they are on the current disk, if they have been Put Away, you cannot access their data. As all active files are held in memory, there could be possible storage problems if you are drawing data from a large number of files, or from a number of large files.

What Was that Name Again?

In practice, the most difficult aspect of creating links between fields is probably that of remembering the names of the fields you want to access. A little bit of discipline goes a long way here. When you are working on a file, make a note of the names and

■ SECTION 34
Files and fields

purposes of key fields. Keep those notes organised and at hand, and creating links between files will be much easier.

For those of us who are less organised, the flip facility (see Section 36) allows us to call up other files and check the names, without having to stop work on the current file.

■ SECTION 35
Linking graphs and spreadsheets

Links can be made into graph files, just as they can to any other part of the Ability system, so a series could be made up of a list of links:

> Series1=+CASHFLOW\jan_gross,+CASHFLOW\feb_gross, +CASHFLOW\mar_gross

It is a method that works well enough if you need to collect scattered values and pull them together in a graph, but it is very long-winded if you want to create a graph from a solid block of data. A better method in this situation is to create a list or range in the spreadsheet, and make a single link between that list and the series.

```
     A       |   B   |   C   |   D   |   E   |   F   |   G   |   H   |   I   |
 1 | Cash Flow Forecast
 2 |
 3 | MONTH            1       2       3       4       5       6       7       8
 4 |
 5 | Gross Profits    0    1000    1000    2000    3000    4000    4000    4000
 6 | Fixed Costs   2500    2500    2500    2500    2500    2500    2500    2500
 7 |
 8 | Net Profit   -2500   -1500   -1500    -500     500    1500    1500    1500
 9 |
10 | Balance      -2500   -4000   -5500   -6000   -5500   -4000   -2500   -1000
11 |
12 |   [gross]    {  gross=(B6..M6) }
13 |   [net]      {  net=(B8..M8) }
14 |   [balance]{  balance=(B10..M10) }
15 |   [titles]  {  titles=(B3..M3) }
```

To graph the key lines of the CASHFLOW spreadsheet – the gross and net profits and the balance, you would start by defining them as ranges on the sheet. Move to an empty field and type in the name and the range:

Enter A12: gross=(B6..M6)

■ SECTION 35
Linking graphs and spreadsheets

The name is then displayed, inside square brackets, in that field to indicate a range definition. As well as marking off data for the series, you can use the same method to handle the graph's labels.

To pull the data across into a graph, include the series name in the reference:

Enter Series1: +CASHFLOW\gross

Enter Labels: +CASHFLOW\titles

■ SECTION 36
Multi-tasking with Flip

Ability's multi-tasking facilities are not as sophisticated as those found in expensive 'windowing' systems, where the screen can be divided into separate areas or windows, with each one running a different program or handling a different file. In Ability, you can only actually see and work on one file at a time, but you can have any number active – and therefore linkable – and you can have a second task close at hand. This is done through flip.

Press **[F9]** – flip and the current task will be suspended; the screen colour will change and you will find yourself back at the Library screen. Down at the right of the status line, the flip message will be showing. Now you can load in a file; do some work; look up that data that you needed for the other task you had been working on. When you want to go back to the earlier job, just press **[F9]** again. After a couple of moments, you will find yourself back exactly where you were. Flip again, and you return to the second task – just where you left off.

Fascinating, you might say, but so what? If you can only work on one task at a time, what is the point of that second flip state? The answer is, that when you start to use flip, you will find that it comes in very useful in four areas – performing odd jobs in the middle of a major piece of work, looking things up, file management and transferring data.

Flip for Odd Jobs

You are heavily into a spreadsheet analysis of the firm's performance over the last year, and you notice that one of the reps has been running up remarkably high expenses. Without further ado, you flip into Write and dash off a memo telling him to see you at once to explain. Then you flip back and complete your analysis.

Another time, you are writing a letter and the telephone rings. It is a potential customer inquiring about prices. You flip, call up your customer database and add his details while you are still on the telephone. You might go on to use the mail-merge functions to print a standard (personalised) letter to accompany the brochure you will be sending. When that is all out of the way, flip back to the letter you had been working on before the call.

■ SECTION 36
Multi-tasking with Flip

Flip for Reference

You want to link a field to one in another file, but not being 100 percent organised, you have not made a note of the names and cannot remember whether it was called 'sales_total','total_sales' or 'sum_sales'. Press flip, load in that other file and look it up. Flip back and make the link.

Flip for File Management

Being 100 percent organised, you have no problem in writing the names to make links between files, but when you enter the reference you get the <N/A> report. The linked file is not active, so Ability cannot get at its data. Flip out, get to the Library screen and load in the other file. If there are several files that need to be active, then you can load each in turn, press **[F10]** to get back to the Library and load the next. As long as the files have been loaded once – and not put-away – they are in memory and can be linked.

You have spent the whole afternoon typing and have at last finished a mammoth report. You press **[F10]** to save and exit, and the system tells you that there is not enough space on the disk for the file! Flip to the Library screen. Scan through the files to see what is no longer needed – there are usually a few redundant files on most people's disks. Erase these until you think there will be enough space for that report. Flip back and see if you can save it this time.

Flip for Data Transfer

You want to pull a table out of a spreadsheet and include it in a report. It would take ages to link the fields in one by one, and you do not need the updating produced by linking. The second alternative – to take the whole spreadsheet in (see the next section) – is not appropriate either, as you only want one small part of a large sheet.

Flip and load in the spreadsheet. Shade the fields that you want to use in your report and press **[F5]** – pick up so that they are held in memory. Flip back to your report and press **[F6]** – put down. The table is written in to your report. (Notice that when you put down data in this way, only the values are transferred – any formulae are lost.)

■ SECTION 37
Graphs and Spreadsheets in Write

One of Ability's very attractive features is that it lets you include graphs and spreadsheets within a Write document. You can pull in existing graphs and spreadsheets, or create new ones, without stopping work on your document. It is a facility that can be particularly useful when producing reports or theses.

Using Existing Graphs

Press [F2] – commands and select graph. At the prompt, type the name of the file. After a moment or two the graph will be drawn at the current cursor position. It will appear to be larger than it is within the graph system, as none of the screen is taken up by series data. Notice though, that when it is printed out, as part of the document, it will be exactly the same size as when printed separately, which is to say, a bit on the small side.

The graph area is marked by highlights on the page borders, and the normal editing facilities do not work within it. You cannot delete a shaded part of the graph, nor insert any additional lines, though the whole graph can be shaded and then picked up or deleted if you decide that you do not want it after all.

The text that is part of the graph cannot be deleted or moved. While it is possible to type over it, this is not usually satisfactory as the original text remains in place underneath. You *can* delete and move any over-written text, and the graph below remains unchanged.

Graphs within documents are not updated automatically. If their series are dependent upon data linked in from a spreadsheet, and that spreadsheet is changed, then the graph will stay the same. If you want the graph redrawn, or if you want to edit its data, add titles or otherwise change the display, you will have to call up the graph commands.

To do this, move the screen cursor into the graph area and press [F2]. Select graph, and this time, instead of asking you for a file name, Ability will offer you a choice of **edit** and **adjust**. Select **edit** and it will be as if you had moved out of Write and into Graph. The label and series area will reappear and the full range of graph commands, including **calc/draw** will be available. When you have finished, [F10] – done takes you back to your document, with an altered, updated graph.

The **adjust** option has a special purpose. With this you can slide the graph from side to side. In the printed version, the display will only occupy about half the width of the page. You may want to centre it in your text, or push it to one side to leave room for comments next to it. As there is a discrepancy between the relative sizes of the graph on screen and paper, it is always a good idea to print out the page containing the graph for checking before you do a full print of the document.

Creating new Graphs

The only real difference here is that after you have typed in the name for the new file, you will be taken directly to the full graph system – just as if you had given the command graph **edit** – so that data can be written for the series.

Whether you have created a new graph, or brought an existing one into the document, the graph is stored on disk as a separate file. All that the Write file contains is a link to that graph file. If you are ever copying Write files from disk to disk, do not forget to copy any linked graph files as well.

Spreadsheets in Write

These are managed in much the same way as graphs. You can use an existing spreadsheet or create a new one. When the cursor is within the area marked by the highlighted borders, the spread-sheet command offers the same edit and adjust options.

There are two main differences from graphs. With a spreadsheet you can opt to load only part of the sheet – if you do this, you will be presented with the full sheet and asked to shade the area you want. Press **[F10]** when you have marked it out.

The second point to note is that the spreadsheet retains its field structure when it is brought into the document. This applies to both full and partial sheets and it means that you can edit or retype the data in individual fields, and that the formulae continue to work. (Obviously, if you have taken only part of the sheet and have left behind some of the fields that are referenced in formulae then there will be errors.) Change any values and the sheet will be recalculated as usual.

■ SECTION 37
Graphs and Spreadsheets in Write

There are also a couple of oddities which can be irritating at times. The first is that if the field has already got data in it, you can use **[F4]** – edit or retype it directly. On the other hand, if the field was empty, then you must use the sequence **[F2] – spreadsheet edit** to enter or edit data.

The other oddity of spreadsheets within Write is in the treatment of long labels within fields. If they will not fit into the available width, they are clipped short, rather than being allowed to overflow into adjacent empty fields. **[F4]** – edit field does not allow you to change the width; this must be done through the spreadsheet commands.

PART SIX

Database

■ SECTION 38
The filing cabinet

Write will certainly replace your typewriter, Spreadsheet will soon take over from your calculator or adding machine. Will Database replace your filing cabinet? The answer is probably yes, but it does depend upon what type of data is stored and what use is made of it.

Database is a general purpose data-handling program. The files produced by this may be referred to as databases, and, within each, information is held as a set of separate records. The database file is therefore the equivalent of a box of record cards. Individual records or groups of related records can be found by getting Database to look for particular attributes; and the whole file can be sorted into order in any number of different ways.

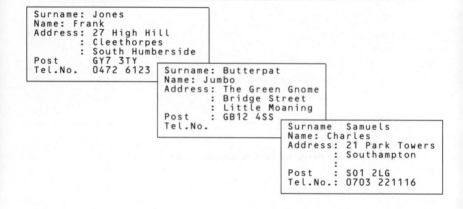

A simple database file might hold the names, addresses and telephone numbers of friends, customers or other contacts. Each person's details would be written on a separate card, or 'form' as Ability calls it, but following a standard layout. This may well mean that there are some blank spaces on some forms — not everyone will have a telephone, and some addresses may need only two lines, while others may need four. The fact that forms have to be able to cope with the biggest entries in each section can make database files rather extravagant in their use of memory.

■ SECTION 38
The filing cabinet

With a normal card-file system, you would sort it into alphabetical order by name, so that you could find cards easily. With Database this is unnecessary. If you need an ordered list of your contacts, you get the system to sort it for you – and it could be sorted by name, address, postcode or telephone number. This flexibility of sorting is matched by an equal flexibility in the ways that you can extract data from the files. You can find Mr Samuels' address and telephone number by setting up a search based on his name, or get a list of all your contacts in South Humberside by basing the search on the county name. Either way, it is the computer that does the searching, and it will find any relevant cards in a matter of moments.

The great advantage of the database system over a card-file is that even though you may sort the file into a new order, or create sub-sets by searching for specific entries – the original file remains intact. Reorganise a card-file, or pull sets of cards out of it, and you are faced with the chore of getting it back into order afterwards.

There are other advantages too, and the most obvious of these must be the possibility of mail-merging. If you want to send a standard letter to all your contacts – or to a selected group of them – then you can draw personal details from your database and incorporate them into the letter. It's very easy to organise and can be a substantial time-saver. Just select the group that are to receive the circular, then specify in the letter which details to include and where to write them, and set it off. The database software will print a set of personalised letters without any further effort on your part.

Personalised mail-shots may have lost their novelty value in recent years, but they are still a good way to get your message across, and mail-merging offers a convenient way to handle routine mailing that might not otherwise be done as often as it should. An end-of-the-month reminder can jog slow payers to reach for their cheque books.

But a word or two about the sizes of files before you start work on Database. Its value, as a means of handling information, grows in direct proportion to the size of the files. It may well be worth its weight in platinum if you have 5,000 customers on your mailing list, but it is often pointless to use it for small jobs.

■ SECTION 38
The filing cabinet

If all you want is to keep names, addresses and telephone numbers for reference only, then you are almost certainly better off with an address book or a card-file, as these are simpler and quicker to use. Database may well be able to find a given name faster than you could look it up in a book, but it takes a minute or two to get Database up and running, while a book is instantly available. A book or a small card-file is also far more portable!

With Write and Spreadsheet, you can learn your way around while you put them to use on limited tasks – letters, memos and short calculations. But with Database, your first proper use of the system is probably going to be on a large application, so there is little chance to learn while you use it. And before you start serious work, there are two questions that must be answered. The first is a purely practical one – is there enough storage space? The second is more a matter of judgement – will it be worth the effort?

How Much Space?

A mail order firm wants to computerise its customer list. For each customer it needs to store several items of data, and the space allocated to each item must be large enough to take the longest possible entry. For example, since there could be people with names such as 'Fotheringay-Robinson', the surname slot must have at least 20 letters – more would be safer. After checking the paper files, the firm might decide on the following allocation of space:

```
Surname              25 characters
Forenames            25 characters
Title                 5 characters
Address       4  *   20 characters
Tel.No.              10 characters
Credit Limit         10 digits      (e.g. 20,000.00 = 9 digits)
Outstanding          10 digits
Invoices      6  *   15 characters (Ref. nos. and dates)
Special Notes        40 characters
```

In total, each customer's record would take approximately 300 bytes of memory. That's about 330 in 100k, and 1,000 customers would need almost 300k of memory. The limits are set by the capacity of the disk storage – not by the available space in the computer's memory. On a floppy disk system, it would be inadvisable to have a database file that took more than 180k, or half a diskful. Any more than this, and it is impossible to back up the file, and difficult to make any use of sub-sets or to write reports. Hard disk systems, with 20 or 40 million bytes of storage, are a rather different matter, but there will still be constraints on space. The database files will not be the only ones on the disk. It is also vital that you should be able to take a back up copy of the file, in case the hard disk fails. So, unless you have a tape backup system, the file will be limited to 360k.

It does not take long to assess your storage needs – just work out how much you need, at most, on each form, and how many forms, at most, you will want to handle. Multiply them together, then double it to allow for some working space. Will the file fit onto a 360k disk, or into the spare memory of the hard disk when all its records have been entered?

Will it be worth it?

The point here is that it takes time and effort to type in a lot of data, and the question is, will it save you time and effort in the long run? If it takes two minutes to type in the details of one record – and that may be an optimistic estimate given that the data will probably need organising at the same time – then, at best, the typist might manage 25 an hour, or 150 to 200 in a day. Allow almost as much time again to check all the records and correct the inevitable scatter of errors. How long will it take to get all the data in?

If the mail-merging functions are going to be used, then the time-saving will soon be apparent. If you regularly need to sort through the file to find records of a particular type – customers with outstanding debts, stock lines that have fallen below reorder levels – then the benefits will be felt fairly quickly. But if the file is only accessed occasionally to look something up or to change a value, then it could be months or years before you recover the time that was spent in creating it.

I make no apologies for dwelling so long on the merits and demerits of databases, but a worthwhile database represents a considerable investment. You must sit down before you start and think carefully how you are going to use it, and whether it is worth doing.

■ SECTION 38
The filing cabinet

The Data Protection Act

Any business, club or society in the UK that maintains a database containing details of identifiable individuals, must register with the Data Protection Registrar, and must allow those individuals access to the data that is held about them. Personnel files, customer accounts and even mailing lists are covered by this law, which can seem a little ridiculous if you only want to store names and addresses but is obviously essential where confidential financial or medical data is concerned. Data is not as secure on a disk as it is in a filing cabinet. Disks are very easy to copy or to steal.

It is a sad reflection on the lack of *glasnost* in our democracy that all government agencies are exempt, and that we have no right to know what files they keep on us.

■ SECTION 39
Setting up a database

Assuming that you have decided that a database would be a good investment, how do you set about creating it?

Organise your Data

The first stage is to take a good look at the data that you are going to use. Let's suppose you wanted to set up an address file of friends and relations so that Christmas cards and party invitations can be handled by mail-merging. Your (disorganised) address book has these details:

> Mr & Mrs S.D. Robinson, 14 The Knoll, Rothwell, Northants, NN14 2EY
>
> Jackie Worthington-Brownall, The Vicarage, Park Road, Leicester, Tel 0533 985674
>
> Dr Christopher Robinson, 27 Gallstone Lane, Highbury, London, N1 3TY, Tel 01-490-2039
>
> Mr Brian Roberts, Flat 21, Woodlands Place, Northlands Road, Southampton, Hants, SO1 2LG, Tel 0703 421116

If we work through this sample, we can see what fields are needed, and how long each must be to take the biggest possible entry.

Field	Width	Longest Entry
Title	8	Mr & Mrs
Forename	11	Christopher
Surname	20	Worthington-Brownall
Address	4 x 15	Various — see below
Postcode	8	NN14 2EY
Tel	11	all

The address fields pose a special problem. Some people have only three-line addresses, while Brian Roberts takes five lines. Allowing five lines for each would leave a lot of unused space in the file. As a compromise, we will allow four fields but increase the width of the first – so that 'Flat 21, Woodlands Place' can be treated as a single entry.

As not everyone in the address book is on our Christmas card list, and fewer are invited to parties, we will also need two fields to handle these. Three characters will do for these as we will only store 'Yes' or 'No' in those fields.

Setting up a database

(It may only have taken a few minutes to sort out the shape of this simple address database, but do not let that lull you into complacency. The time it takes to organise data grows geometrically with the amount of data. If you have twice as much to organise, it takes four times as long – ten times as much data could take 100 times as long!)

Make a Form

Having organised our data, the next job is to create the master form on which the records are to be written. The make a form screen displays a blank form, with a cross-hatched border around it, like a small page from Write. The similarity is intentional, for the operations here are almost identical to Write.

The text handling is the same. The normal Write function keys and commands are available; you can centre text and set typestyles, change the page-format, shade areas and move them around, just as with any ordinary document. Type in the text that you want to appear as headings and comments on the forms of your database. After you have written each heading, set up a field next to it for its data.

Fields are managed in a slightly different way than in Write. When you call up the field command you will be asked for a name, and then required to set the width. This cannot be left undefined, as in a Write document. It must be big enough to take in whatever data may be typed there later, though it may not occupy more than a single line. If you want a four-line address, you need four fields. (Do not be too generous in your widths, as the unused spaces in the fields will also be stored on the disk.)

For the address database, we might use these names and widths:

```
title        8
forename    11
surname     20
address_1   25
address_2   15
address_3   15
address_4   15
postcode    10
tel         11
xmas         3
invite       3
```

Setting up a database

It does not apply in this example, but if a field is to store numbers, you may want to format it. To do this, set the cursor on the field, so that **[F4]** — edit field becomes active, then select the format option.

You can also use edit field to change the name or the width later, while you are still in the **make a form** routine.

```
                              ADDRESS FILE
   Surname   :[              ]        Title :[       ]

   Forename  :[          ]

   Address   :[                  ]
             :[               ]
             :[               ]
             :[               ]
   Post Code :[        ]          Tel.No.    :[         ]
   Xmas Card :[    ]              Invitation :[    ]

   DB ADDRESS;Make a form    Page 1  Line 16  Col 2    93% Free

   F1 — Help      F3 — Goto   F5 — Pick Up  F7 — Shade
   F2 — Commands               F6 — Put Down F8 — Calc/Draw F10 — Done
```

FIGURE 39-1 The master form

You do not have to have a heading for each field — in the example in Figure 39.1 the four fields that have been defined for the address only have the one heading, though they do have different names. Text is decorative. It is there only to make the form easier to use.

While it will normally be most convenient to include all the fields in a single page, there is nothing to stop you from designing a form that has two or more pages. The first would be the most visible one and should contain the key data items; subsequent pages can be used as continuation sheets.

■ SECTION 39
Setting up a database

When you have defined all the fields that you want, and are satisfied with the layout of the form, press **[F10]** to save it. It is always as well to get the form right first time, but no disaster if you do not. If you discover, after you have begun entering data, that you have forgotten a field, or that the master form needs altering in any way, you can redefine it without losing the data you have typed in.

Formulae in Forms

The fields in Database, as elsewhere in the system, may contain calculations and formulae. The master form for a stock control file, shown in Figure 39.2, has these field definitions:

Order Now? = (no_in_stock < reorder)
Stock Value = no_in_stock * unit_price

The 'order now?' field contains a logical test. If the number in stock is below the reorder level, then that field will display a '1', otherwise it will show '0'. You will see later how this field can be used to extract a list of items that need to be reordered.

```
                       STOCK DATABASE
Ref.No.   :[        ]  Category :[            ]

Description  :[                         ]

Supplier Ref :[                  ]

No. in Stock   :[        ]  Reorder Level :[      ]

Order Quantity :[        ]  Order Now? : [ ] ( 1 = Yes )

Unit Cost      :[        ]  Selling Price   :[      ]

Stock Value    :[        ]  Annual Usage    :[      ]
─────────────────────────────────────────────────────────
DB ADDRESS;Sort        Choose sort criteria       93% Free

F1 — Help
F2 — Commands    F4 — Edit Field               F10 — Done
```

FIGURE 39-2 A form for stock control

■ SECTION 40
Entering data

Adding Forms

When you exit from **make a form**, you will be taken directly to **add forms** so that you can start to type in the data.

Note that the order in which you enter the records is irrelevant. Ability has no need of an index or an alphabetical arrangement to help it to find a form; but if you need it sorted – perhaps to get an organized print-out, then that can be done later. Nor is it necessary to type in the whole data file at one sitting – new forms can be added at any time afterwards. It is worth while taking the time to check for errors. While it is simple enough to correct them afterwards, it is far easier to spot mistakes and correct them before entry.

Data is entered into fields, and the fields are handled here just as they are elsewhere in Ability. When the cursor highlights a field, you can type new data into it or press **[F4]** to edit the existing entry. Press **[F10]** – done when the form has been filled in and checked. The fields will then be cleared and the next form can be written.

If data is entered into the wrong field, it can be typed over, or erased by entering a space. Where there are a lot of wrong entries on a record, it may be quicker to wipe all the fields at once by pressing **[F2]** and using the **clear** command. (This is the only command available – or needed – in the add forms routine.)

```
                      ADDRESS FILE
  Surname    :[Robinson           ]      Title :[Dr.    ]

  Forename   :[Christopher]

  Address    :[27 Gallstone Lane        ]
             :[Highbury         ]
             :[London           ]
             :[                 ]
  Post Code :[N1 3TY  ]            Tel.No.    :[01-490-2039]
  Xmas Card :[Yes]                 Invitation :[    ]

  DB ADDRESS;Add forms                           92% Free
  Enter invite :No
  F1 — Help
  F2 — Commands  F4 — Edit Field               F10 — Done
```

FIGURE 40-1 Address form in use

■ SECTION 40
Entering data

Where an entry is too long to fit into a field, the system will appear to accept it. Be warned, this is a temporary state of affairs! When you look back at that entry, after you have finished adding forms, you will find that the entry has been cropped to the length of the field.

When you have done for the day, press **[F10]** to enter the last form, then press **[F10]** again to exit from the add forms routines.

You can end pressing **[Esc]**, but note that if you do this, the data on the current form will be lost.

However you leave this routine, you will be taken to the **browse** part of the system.

■ SECTION 41
Browsing and updating files

The **browse** screen is where you will normally start when you load in a Database file, and it is here that the day-to-day work of searching, sorting and updating the file is performed.

You can browse through the file, form by form, to look for information or to edit entries. Movement is controlled mainly by the [Pg..] keys:

```
        [PgDn] — go to next form
        [PgUp] — go to previous form
[Ctrl] [PgUp] — go to start of first form
[Ctrl] [PgDn] — go to last form
```

In practice, browsing is a poor way to get information out of a large file, and you would only normally use it after you have produced a restricted group of forms with the **make-subset** command. Flicking backwards and forwards through a small set is quite a different matter.

[F3] – goto offers two alternative ways of getting round the file: **search** and **form**. Use the second option if you know the number of the form that you want – an unlikely event in a large database. The **search** option is far more useful, but more complex. We will look at that along with other ways of finding information from the file in the next section.

Editing Entries

As you browse through a file you can correct errors or rewrite the entries on the current form – the one that you can see. Use the arrow keys to move between fields, then either retype the contents or use **[F4]** – edit field to edit them. That's all there is to it.

Deleting Forms

Press **[.Del]** and the current form will be deleted from the file – subject to your confirmation. When a form has been deleted, it will not be displayed as you browse through the file, and will be ignored in sort and search operations, but it is not actually removed. The data remains on file until it is removed permanently by **backup**. Until that time, any form that has been deleted in the current, or in previous, working sessions can be brought back into use by **recover**. (See over.)

■ SECTION 41
Browsing and updating files

The data on the current form can be edited, or the whole form deleted from the file at any time. This is a bit of a two-edged sword, as it means that anyone who is allowed access to the file can corrupt its data, either intentionally or accidentally. For this reason, you should always have a backup copy of the file on another disk, locked safely away.

The Browse Commands

Add forms

The routine is exactly the same as when first starting the database. The new forms will be added to the end of the file.

Change

If you always think through your databases properly, and anticipate all possible problems before designing the forms, you will never need to use this command. However, we all make the odd mistake, and it is not possible to anticipate all eventualities, so be glad that change is there, for it allows you to alter the structure of the master form.

It starts by asking you for a file name, for this routine will create a new file, containing all existing data but reorganised to fit into the new form structure. Alterations can then be made via a routine which is all but identical to **make a form**. Add or delete individual fields, rearrange the layout and adjust the format or width of fields. When you have finished, press **[F10]**. The system will then save the new master form and copy all the data across into the new file. (You can erase the old version of the database at the end of your working session, if you no longer need it.)

Printing a form

Press **[F2]** and select **print** from the command menu to get a paper copy of the current form, as it appears on screen. If you want to print a set of forms, then use the report command. (See Section 44.)

Recover

Get to the deleted forms by calling up **recover** and browsing through them with [PgUp] and [PgDn] until you find the ones you want. Press **[Ins]** to reinsert a form into the file.

Browsing and updating files

(There's an odd little bug that you might occasionally meet as you try to exit from this routine. Either **[F10]** or **[Esc]** will normally take you back to **browse**, but in some circumstances you can seem to be trapped inside **recover**. When this happens, press **[F2]** and select **recover**. That lets you out, but don't ask me why it works!)

Backup

This command creates a backup copy of the file, complete with deleted forms, and a new working copy free from those deleted forms. It is probably of most use where there is a high turnover of records and the file gets cluttered up with unwanted data. The new slim version will take up less disk space and will be marginally quicker to sort and search.

The backup copy will have the same name, but with a **.BAK** extension, and will be displayed under the **OTHER FILES** heading on the Library screen. It is possible to recover the deleted forms from this copy, but not normally worth the effort. For a start you would have to reverse the backup process – by erasing the current working copy and renaming the .BAK file to give it a **.XDB** extension. (All Database files have .XDB after their names, but the extension is not shown on the Library screen.)

If you have edited or added to your current working copy before you discover that there are forms that you want to recover, then the process is scarcely worth the effort as you will lose the new alterations. Far better to go through the file before using Backup, recovering any forms that you might possibly want in future. They can then be deleted from the new working copy, but will still be at hand if needed.

Validate

This is a special purpose command, of use only where one or more of the fields contain formulae that draw on values written into a spreadsheet. The stock control database, for example, could be extended to include two prices for each item – with and without VAT. The tax is currently 15 percent, but it could change and it would be terribly time-consuming to have to work through every form recalculating the VAT-inclusive price. The solution is to write the VAT percentage into a spreadsheet, and to draw on this in the database formula.

    incvat = price * stockref\vat

Browsing and updating files

To update the **incvat** value in all forms, you would only need to retype the percentage in the **vat** field of the **stockref** spreadsheet, then give the **validate** command when you are back in the database.

All calculations take a little time, so if the database contains hundreds of forms, validating may take a minute or two.

From Database to Spreadsheet

Where there is a lot of numeric data and calculations have to be made, it may be useful to copy the data into a spreadsheet and perform the calculations there. This can be done very easily.

1 Press **[F5]** – this picks up the whole file, not just the current form.

2 Press **[F9]** – flip and start a new spreadsheet.

3 Press **[F6]** – and put down the file inside the spreadsheet.

4 Each form will take a row of the sheet, with a field to each column.

The data can be picked up and put down back into the database as long as the number and arrangements of fields has not been changed. When copying this way, shade the area containing the data before pressing **[F5]**.

■ SECTION 42
Searching and making subsets

The **search** routine is essentially the same here as in the spreadsheet part of the system. It simply searches through the file looking for the **next** or **previous** form where there is matching data. When a match is found, you can escape from the search and use or alter the found data. The only significant difference is that in Database the search can be looking for two or more criteria on each form.

If we were searching our address file for Brian Roberts' details, his surname would be the only necessary criterion; if we wanted Dr Christopher Robinson's form, and there are several Robinsons in our file, then the forename or title would also be needed in the definition. On the stock control file, by looking for those forms where the 'order now?' field contains '1', we could find those items that had fallen below reorder level.

When you use the **make-subset** command, those forms that match the given criteria are marked off to form a new set, just as if you had pulled cards out of a box-file and stacked them by the side. This sub-set can then be browsed, stored on disk as a new file by the **write** command, or printed out by **report**. In the address file, an obvious subset to make would be of those people to whom party invitations are sent. This group could then be processed through the **mail-merge** routine to produce personal letters of invitation.

If you want, you can take a new selection from the group by using **make-subset** again. (The process can be repeated as often as you like, to make subsets of subsets of subsets!) So, the first subset from a customer file might be of those owing money; a second level subset could then focus on those owing more than a certain amount.

The advantage of the database over a paper-file is very apparent here. If you have physically removed cards from a box, you have to sort them all back into place again. The **make-subset** command does not actually remove anything, and the file can be restored to normal in a jiffy.

Defining Criteria

Whether you are **searching** for an individual form, or using **make-subset** to select a group of related forms, the process starts at the same point.

■ SECTION 42
Searching and making subsets

You are presented with a screen on which to write the criteria that define the forms that you want to isolate. (The status line will carry the message **search for** or **pick subset**, but the routine is identical.) When it is first used, this form will be blank. On subsequent use, the previous criteria will be displayed. This can be useful where you want to select a smaller group out of a subset. For a fresh start, press **[F2]** and use the **clear** command.

Define your criteria, as detailed below, and press **[F10]** when you have done. On a search, you will then be asked to choose between **next** and **previous** as with searches elsewhere.

Within the **make-subset** command, the system will grind for a few moments while it selects the forms, then switch you back into browse. The **(subset)** in the status line tells you that you are browsing within a selected group of forms.

Fixed Criteria

Where you want something definite, type it in to the appropriate field. To find Roberts, type 'Roberts' into the surname field. (It does not matter about capitals or lower case, they are ignored. 'ROBERTS', 'Roberts' and 'roberts' will all find the same form.)

Press **[F10]** and the system will then find all the forms where the surname is Roberts.

Making Comparisons

If the fields contain numbers, the *relational operators* can be used to make comparisons. For example, in a customer accounts file you could find those who owed more then £500 by typing > **500** into the 'owing' field. Similarly <= **100** would pick up those smaller debts up to and including £100.

The relational operators are:

```
> more than            >= more than or equal to
< less than            <= less than or equal to
~= or <> not equal to
```

■ SECTION 42
Searching and making subsets

Using Wildcards

Wildcards (or 'jokers' as they are usually called this side of the Atlantic) are cards which can be used in place of any other. In Ability there are two characters which can be used in place of any other characters. They are the same two that are used in MS-DOS commands.

* The asterisk stands for any number of other characters. Type **R***
  into the surname field of an address file and the search will find
  any surname beginning with 'R' – Robinson, Roberts, Rath-
  bone, Rex. The length is immaterial.

? The question mark stands for a single unknown character. Did
  that distant cousin live in Lancashire or Lincolnshire? Type
  L?ncs into the right field and both 'Lincs' and 'Lancs' will match.

Using Logical Operators

AND (**&**) and OR(│) can be used to join two conditions within a single field. They would have little purpose in our simple address file, but can be very valuable in more complex databases. The salesman organising his itinerary to the West Country might want to get a list of customers who live in either Devon OR Cornwall. The criterion for the 'County' field would be written:

Devon │ Cornwall

The credit controller, to get a list of those owed between £100 AND £1,000, would enter this into the 'outstanding' field:

>=500 & <=1000

Multiple Criteria

If you wanted to select a group on the basis of multiple criteria, for example those Robinsons that you include in your party invitations, you can go about it in two ways. Either make the subset in stages, or define all the criteria at the start.

To do it in stages, first define one criterion – give Robinson as the surname – press **[F10]** and let the system get that set together. Then call up **make-subset** again, leave the 'Robinson' in the surname field and type 'Yes' in the invitation field. Press **[F10]** and the second level subset will be selected by the system.

Searching and making subsets

The alternative is to type both criteria into the form at the beginning and make the subset in a single operation. This is the quickest way to do it, but working in stages does give you a chance to browse as you work through.

Restoring the File

To get back from a subset to the original file, select **make-subset** and use the **clear** command to erase all criteria. Press **[F10]** to complete the operation. As there are no limiting criteria, the whole file will be selected as the 'subset'.

In practice, you rarely need to bother about restoring the file. It is not necessary to do this before selecting a new subset, as the whole file will always be searched for matching forms. Nor is it necessary to restore the file before closing down at the end of the session. The subsets are only temporary, and are not saved. Next time you load in that file, it will be there in full.

Saving a Subset

The **Write** command will create a new file containing only those files that are in the current subset, should you need a permanent copy. A club secretary, for example, might use this to split the membership file into current and lapsed members. The process would start by making a subset of those who had not renewed their membership. Those forms would then be stored in a new file, using Write. A second subset, of those who had renewed, would then be made and written to disk. At the end of the session, when back in the Library screen, the original file could be renamed as 'OLDFILE', transferred to another disk or directory for permanent storage, then erased from the working disk.

■ SECTION 43

Sorted files

The **sort** command can be used to arrange the forms into order, based on the contents of any of the fields. With some types of file there is only one type of order that makes sense – that address file might be usefully sorted into surname order, but there would be little point in sorting it any other way. Our sample forms would then be arranged:

Mr Brian Roberts.....
Mr & Mrs S.D. Robinson.....
Dr Christopher Robinson.....
Jackie Worthington-Brownall.....

Other files need to be sorted in different ways for different uses. A customer account file might be sorted into order of turnover, so that the best customers could be easily identified; while sorting by outstanding bills will show up the biggest debtors.

The sort can be based on more than one field. That address file contains several people with the same surname, so it would be better sorted first by surname, then by forename.

Mr Brian Roberts.....
Dr Christopher Robinson.....
Mr & Mrs S.D. Robinson.....
Jackie Worthington-Brownall.....

Sorting is not just for producing ordered lists. It can also be used for gathering forms into categories. Sort a club file by type of membership, and it will be grouped into committee, junior, ordinary and retired. The stock control file sorted first by category and then by description would give an alphabetical list within each type of stock.

When Ability sorts a database file it does not actually change the order of the forms. Instead it makes an index, and stores that on the disk. (None of this is apparent from the outside. The forms are displayed on screen in their sorted order, and the name of the index is listed with the ordinary files beneath the database heading on the Library screen.)

The method has two very significant advantages. The sorted file takes up very little disk space, as all it holds is a list of form numbers; and you can have as many different indices or arrangements of the file as you like. At the start of a session you can load in the file either by its original name, or the name of a sorted version.

There are also some drawbacks. You cannot add forms to the sorted file, or delete them, nor can you sort it again along different lines. To do any of these, you have to close down the file, go back to the Library screen and load in the original, unsorted file.

Note that when you use **backup** on a file, the indices will be erased from the disk as they will no longer be correct. You will therefore need to sort again after backing up.

Organising a Sort

When you select **sort**, you will be presented with a blank form. For a simple sort, just type '**1**' in the chosen field and exit by pressing **[F10]**. The file will then be sorted in ascending order, based on the items in that field.

Where the sort is to be on more than one field, type the order of importance into the fields. In the example here, the file is to be sorted first by surname, then by forename.

```
                         ADDRESS FILE
   Surname    :[1                 ]       Title :[       ]

   Forename   :[2          ]

   Address    :[                       ]
              :[             ]
              :[             ]
              :[             ]
   Post Code :[        ]            Tel.No.    :[         ]
   Xmas Card :[    ]                Invitation :[    ]

   DB ADDRESS;Sort          Choose sort criteria       93% Free

   F1 — Help
   F2 — Commands    F4 — Edit Field                    F10 — Done
```

FIGURE 43-1 Sorting on two fields

Descending Order

If the file is to be sorted into descending order — you might want the customer file arranged with those owing most at the top of the list — type the letter '**d**' after the number.

Amount Owing :[1d   ]

■ SECTION 43
Sorted files

Using the Sorted File

It takes Ability remarkably little time to sort a file. It can, for instance, arrange 500 forms into order in less than three minutes. When it has finished, you will be returned to the browse screen, but this time you will see an asterisk (*) after the file name to remind you that it is a sorted file.

The sorted file can be browsed, searched and its forms edited in just the same way as an unsorted one. However, no major alterations are possible, so the only three [F2] commands that can be used here are **Make-subset**, **Write** and **Report**. This is reasonable. The only real purpose of a Sort is so that the file, or a subset of it, can be printed out in an organised list.

■ SECTION 44
Reporting out

In Write and the Spreadsheet, **print** is a full-function command. In the Database, **print** is no more than a handy utility for getting the odd paper copy of a form. Here all the serious printing is handled via the **report** command with its three options – forms, summary and mail-merge. All work on either the whole file or a subset if one is currently in use.

Forms

The main output option here is **printer**, which prints out all the forms, just as they appear on the screen, with each form on a new page.

The alternative **view** simply displays the forms on screen. As you can achieve exactly the same result by browsing through one page at a time, I fail to see the purpose of this.

Summary

This is far more useful, for it allows you to get a printed summary of the database, with one line for each form and containing only those fields that you want to see at that time. Not only that, the routine can also work out totals of numeric fields, and even sub-totals of related groups.

The style and layout of the summary is stored on disk, so that it can be reused in future. (Note that this refers to the format *only* and not to the data that is included in the report.) This can be a valuable time-saver with accounts or other databases where regular reports are needed.

The first step in producing the summary is to give the name of the report format file – if any exist already, their names will be displayed on the screen.

Reporting out

```
                         ADDRESS FILE
Surname    :[ 3               ]        Title :[ 1      ]

Forename   :[ 2           ]

Address    :[                     ]
           :[              ]
           :[              ]
           :[              ]
Post Code  :[         ]            Tel.No.    :[ 4        ]
Xmas Card  :[    ]                 Invitation :[     ]
───────────────────────────────────────────────────────────
DB ADDRESS;Sort         Choose sort criteria      93% Free

F1 — Help
F2 — Commands    F4 — Edit Field                   F10 — Done
```

FIGURE 44-1 Selecting fields for summary report

The next stage is to define which fields are to be included in the summary, and in what order they should be written. This is done by writing the order of printing onto a blank form, as shown in Figure 44.1. In that example, the report lines would look like this:

```
Mr   Brian       Roberts          0703 421116
Dr   Christopher Robinson         01-490-2039
```

Note the spacing. Each field is given its full width, no matter how many blank spaces it contains. This does ensure that the data is aligned, but wide fields can produce long gaps that make the summary less easy to read. Keep an eye on the total number of characters. If the field widths add up to more than 80, then you will have to use the Elite or Condensed typeface when printing.

Adding Headings

If you want to add headings to the top of each printed column, then these should be written into the fields after the order number, separated by a comma. Examples are shown in Figure 44.2.

Reporting out

Totals

Where the fields contain numbers, Ability can total them up as it works through the file and print the total at the end of the report. To do this, write a **t** after the print order number. On the stock control file, we could get a valuation by totalling the stock values.

```
                       STOCK DATABASE


  Ref.No.   :[          ]  Category :[ 1b,Category ]

  Description  :[ 2,Description          ]

  Supplier Ref :[                   ]

  No. in Stock   :[ 3,Number]   Reorder Level :[       ]

  Order Quantity :[         ]   Order Now? : [5,Reorder Now ]

  Unit Cost      :[        ]   Selling Price   :[         ]

  Stock Value    :[ 4t,Value]   Annual Usage    :[         ]

  DB ADDRESS;Sort         Choose sort criteria        93% Free

  F1 — Help
  F2 — Commands    F4 — Edit Field                     F10 — Done
```

FIGURE 44-2 Summary report with headings

Breaks

If a file has been sorted into categories, you can set the report to leave a line break whenever the contents of a field change. If other fields are being totalled, then sub-totals will be printed at each break. To set the breaks, type **b** into the category field.

A stock control file for a DIY store might classify its stock into Building, Doors, Paint, Timber, Tools and Windows. If the file was sorted by category, then breaks requested in the summary, the report would print a list of all Building items, then leave a gap before starting on the Doors.

You can see breaks, totals and headings all in use in the example in Figure 44.2. You will note that five fields are to be included in the summary and that all have been given headings. The 'category' field has the **b** option, and the 'value' field has the **t** option. When this report is printed, the stock lines will be grouped by type, with value sub-totals beneath, and an overall total at the end of the report. (Figure 44.3.)

```
                           STOCK DATABASE

Category          Description             Number   Value      Reorder Now
Timber            2 x 4 PAR 8'            12       24.00      1
Timber            2 x 2 PAR 8'            20       17.40      0
.....             .....                   ..       .....      .
Timber            0.75 x 1.5 PAR 6'       60       21.60      0
                                                   780.50

Tools             Trowel, pointing        5        12.35      0
Tools             Trowel, brick           3        13.10      1
.....             .....                   ..       .....      ..
Tools             Hammer,16oz claw        4         8.16      1
                                                   368.29
                                                 3,286.74
```

FIGURE 44-3 The report output

Printing the Report

When the report definition has been completed, press **[F10]** to end. The routine will then save the format before moving on to the print options. All the normal options are available – you may find the **cpi** one particularly useful, as the Elite or Condensed mode typefaces will squeeze nearly 100, or over 130, characters into the line, respectively.

■ SECTION 45
Mail-merging

We have seen already how Ability's integration facilities allow you to draw data from one file to use in another. Mail-merging is an extension of this. Selected data is drawn from a database and combined into a standard letter or report, so that a personalised document is produced for each form in the file or subset.

You may mail-merge into an existing Write document, or create a new one from within the Database part of the software. At the start of the routine, Ability will ask you for a filename, and, if the file does not exist on the current disk, it will assume that you want to type a new one. The word-processing routine that is then called up is identical to Write.

You must give the *full* names of the database fields when referring to them in the document – even when the document is being written within Database. Thus a circular letter that is to be merged with data from a file called 'NAMES' might start with field references such as these:

> +names\title +names\initials +names\surname
> +names\address1
> +names\address2
> +names\address3

> **Dear !in_title !in_surname**

> **I thought you might be interested to know that** . . . .

Note those two-way links after the 'Dear'. When you are mail-merging, you can only use each item of data from the database once. If you want to use the same data twice, you have to set up the second link inside the document. In this example, the first field in the document (containing the reference +**names\title**) will have been named **in_title**. It is this field that is drawn upon by the **!in_title** reference after the word 'Dear'. In the same way, the third field in the top line will have been named **in_surname** so that its data can be used again later.

■ SECTION 45
Mail-merging

Watch out for field widths when mail-merging! When the database field is printed within the document, it will take up its full width – including any trailing spaces. This will make no difference to the appearance when the field is printed on its own – as in the headings of a letter – but can cause problems if the field is embedded in the text. Where this is required, the document's field should have its width set to match that of the database. If you leave the width undefined, any text to the right could be pushed off the edge when printed!

Label printing is not possible with Ability, unless you are prepared to print only one label on every page. The mail-merge routine always starts a new page for every database form.

PART SEVEN

Communicate

■ SECTION 46
Communication files

Let's get it clear from the start that in this case Ability is not enough by itself. You cannot use the Communicate software without some extra hardware. At the very least this will consist of an RS232 cable, where you want to link two computers together within the same office, although in this situation it could well be easier to pass disks to one another. To communicate with the world beyond, you will need a modem. (For the non-technically minded, this is the electronic gizmo that converts computer signals into a form suitable for transmission on the telephone lines, and vice versa.)

The type of modem is not important as long as it is Hayes-compatible – and most are. Cheap and cheerful models cost around £50, while a good quality unit can run to over £200. Some are in the form of a box that sits between the computer and the telephone, others are on cards that are slotted into the body of the PC. None are difficult to set up, though you may need to have one of the new telephone sockets installed by BT.

Generally speaking, the higher priced modems have greater flexibility, which can be worth having as the telecommunications industry is still struggling slowly towards standardisation. There is an awful lot of variation in the styles and speeds that computers use when they talk to each other.

Once you have got the modem wired up, you will be able to communicate with the amateur bulletin boards and with any other Ability user. If you want to make fuller use of the system, you will then need to join one of the national communications networks such as Telecom Gold or Micronet. Through these you can gain access to a substantial range of information and communication services. Your computer could then be used as a telex terminal; via electronic mail you could communicate instantly with other users throughout the UK and abroad; using the Jordans or Infocheck database, you could check up on the status and credit ratings of potential business customers before committing yourself to a deal; up-to-the-minute financial, national and international news are readily available; you can even book a rail ticket or a theatre seat!

■ SECTION 46
Communication files

Of course, little of this is free. There is a membership fee for these networks, telephone time must be paid for (though usually at local rates), and the specialist database services all charge for their use. But it is well worth exploring. A great many firms have already found that the improved communications and easy access to information offer very significant cost-benefits.

Setting Up a Communicate File

Each link that you make is handled by a separate file, in which will be stored the telephone number and details of any special settings, passwords and such. So, if you communicated with Telecom Gold, a branch office and a bulletin board, you might have files called TELECOM, BRANCH and BULLET. To start a new file, point to << NEW >> on the Library screen and type its name. Communicate will then start up.

One of the most remarkable features of Communicate's working screen is its almost complete absence of features! It is blank apart from the function key reminders at the bottom. Do not worry, it will fill up later as you get into the session, as everything that you type, or that the other computer sends to you, will be displayed on that screen.

When you open a new file, the first job is to fix the **port** and **terminal** settings. Together these determine how your computer will communicate with the one at the other end of the telephone line.

Port

This command handles your end of the communication. It calls up the screen shown in Figure 46.1. The default settings should be right for most purposes, so it may be that no work is necessary here.

The one thing that you must check is that you are using the right **communications port**. The Amstrad PC has two, labelled **COM1** and **COM2**, and the modem can be connected to either. To change this, or any other setting on the screen, position the cursor on the field and press **[Enter]**.

The **baud rate** refers to the speed at which data is sent and received. 1200 baud is the rate most commonly used, though many bulletin boards run at 300 baud.

■ SECTION 46
Communication files

Parity refers to the way that the computer checks that data is being received correctly. The most common alternatives here are **none**, **odd** and **even**.

Few of the other settings will ever need changing. If a network does use non-standard settings, they will let you know what they should be.

When you have checked the screen, press **[F10]** to save the settings.

```
                        COMMUNICATION SETTINGS
===============================================================

Communication Port  [COM1    ]   Parity             [None    ]

Baud Rate           [    1200]   Duplex             [Full    ]

Character Size      [      8]    Stop Bits          [       1]


Local Linefeed      [No      ]   Remote Linefeed    [Yes     ]

Local FLow Control  [XON/XOFF]   Remote Flow Control [XON/XOFF]

Send Break          [Yes     ]   Break Character    [ff      ]
---------------------------------------------------------------
Communicate: MICLINK                      87% Free

F1 — Help
                                          F10 — Done
```

FIGURE 46-1 The Port screen

Terminal

This command brings you to the terminal and modem settings screen (Figure 46.2). As with the port settings, you should find that few of the values need changing – certainly not for Telecom Gold, Micronet or for communicating with another Ability user.

■ SECTION 46
Communication files

Only one entry is always essential for telecommunications. You must type in the telephone number! This can be written as a single string of digits, or with spaces or dashes between the sets. '015831200', '01 583 1200' and '01-583-1200' will all work just as well, although the latter two are more readable. If the computer is to be used in an office where you have to dial a digit first to get an outside line, then include one or more commas in the number. The system will wait for two seconds for every comma. So, to allow four seconds for the outside line to be put through, the number might be written '9,,01-583-1200'.

```
                    TERMINAL AND MODEM SETTINGS

    Terminal Type      [VT100   ]   Modem Type        [Hayes   ]

    Line Wrap          [Yes     ]   Page Mode         [Scroll  ]

    Screen Length      [21 lines]   Reverse Video     [No      ]

    Answer on Ring #   [1       ]   Dialing Method    [Pulse   ]

    Transmit Password  [--------]   Receive Password  [--------]

    Login File         [----------] Transfer Protocol [Xmodem  ]

    Phone Number       [01-583-1200                            ]


Communicate: MICLINK                      87% Free
Enter : ------
F1 - Help
            F4 - Edit Field                      F10 - Done
```

FIGURE 46-2 The Terminal screen

Where you are making a direct link between two machines, then there will, of course, be no telephone number. But in this case you would need to change the **modem type**. Point to it and press **[Enter]** until **none** appears in the field.

The **transmit** and **receive passwords** come into play when you are communicating with another Ability user, when they will provide some measure of security. When two Ability users are communicating, each can have open access to the files of the other. To prevent abuse of this openness, your **receive password** must match the other user's **transmit password** or you will not be allowed to copy files from that system.

■ SECTION 46
Communication files

As you will see below, when you are expecting a communication from another user, you can leave the software running and get it to answer the telephone for you. The **answer on ring** # number controls how many times the telephone will ring before Communicate makes the connection.

Login Files

The Login File allows you to automate the signing on procedure at the start of a session on a network or bulletin board. If nothing else, it can save you the trouble of looking up your user number and password every time. To use this, you would first create a file, with Write, using the keywords **SEND** and **WAIT**. SEND precedes the text you want to send, and WAIT will make the system wait for a given prompt from the host computer – the one at the other end of the line.

For example, a typical connection sequence to Microlink (a section of Telecom Gold), might run like this:

```
Prompt              Reply

PAD>                CALL 74
Please Sign On
>                   ID SCK123
Password:           LETMEIN
```

To automate this, you would create a file, which might be called LINKLOG, that would look like this:

> **WAIT PAD>**
> **SEND CALL 74**
> **WAIT >**
> **SEND ID SCK123**
> **WAIT Password:**
> **SEND LETMEIN**

The name LINKLOG would then be written into the terminal screen as the **login file** for Microlink. When you give the **call** command, it will make the telephone call. Then, when the connection is made, it will run through the login file's sequence.

Once the port and terminal screens have been adjusted to suit, the first call can be made. If you do not want to do this at the time, press **[F10]** to exit. Next time you load in that Communicate file, the system will have all the data it needs to be able to make a call straightaway.

■ SECTION 47
The on-line commands

Let's turn now to those Communicate commands that are used in a communication session. These are the ones that will make the connections, and handle the transfer of data between your computer and the one at the other end of the line.

Modem – Call

This starts the ball rolling. If you turn up the volume a little on your computer, you should be able to hear it dialling, and to hear the other computer answering. This latter sound is normally something of a high-pitched crackle or tremulous whine. When the connection is made, there will usually be a pause for a moment or so before the other computer's greeting or login message appears on your screen. What happens next depends upon whom you are calling.

If a connection cannot be made, Communicate will usually abandon the attempt after a while and give a 'NO COMPUTER ANSWERED' message. If you hit problems that the system cannot cope with, press [Esc] to break out. There may be a bit of a time lapse before you see any response. Everything slows down a bit when you are communicating.

Modem – Hangup

Use this at the end of the session to disconnect the telephone – and if you have been linked into a commercial database, for heaven's sake remember to log off first. They charge you for the time that you are logged on to their network!

Modem – Answer

When you are expecting a call from another Ability user, select this command and leave Communicate running. When the other user rings, the system will answer the telephone and establish the connection for you. Use **modem – noanswer** afterwards to restore normal service on the telephone line.

■ SECTION 47
The on-line commands

Working On-Line and Off-Line

Where you want to read an incoming file, or write text to send to the other computer, you can usually do so either on-line or off-line. **On-line** means that you read the file as it comes in, or write it while you are connected. This is fine for short pieces of text, but can be very expensive in telephone bills for anything of any length.

Working **off-line**, you would copy incoming data directly into a disk file to read later at your leisure, or Write your text before you start, then send the file down the line during the session. It is far cheaper to work this way whenever you can. Working at 1200 baud, the computer can transfer over 20 words a second – can you read or write that fast?

Capture

Use this to copy incoming data onto a file. When you give the command for the first time, you will be asked for a file name. Everything that comes in will then be written into this file until you use the **capture** command again to end the filing. During a single session you can set up as many different capture files as you need.

At the end of the session, those files can be loaded into Write for reading or editing.

Capture can also be used for monitoring the computer when it is left unattended in **answer** mode. If other Ability users call up to send or receive files, their commands and the system's responses will all be recorded in the capture file.

List

This sends a file down the line. The file must be on the disk in the active drive, or in the current directory. Once you have given the file name, there is nothing else to do until it has finished sending the data.

Send and Receive

These are used for data transfer between Ability users only. They are both used in much the same way, and both allow the transfer of **single** or **many** files at a time.

To **send** a file, all that is necessary is that the connection has been made, the named file is on the current disk or directory, and there is sufficient storage space available at the other end. The second user does not have to do anything – indeed, he should not do anything while data is being sent.

Likewise **receive** requires no operations from the other end, merely that the named file is present in that user's current disk. Its name may imply a passivity, but this is an active command. When you tell Ability to **receive**, it goes out and gets the file that you have named.

The only restriction here is if passwords have been written into the terminal settings. Then your receive password must correspond to the other's transmit. (Note that the passwords apply to access in general, not to a particular file. If you have files that you do not want your Ability co-communicators to receive, then do not tell them their names, or, better still, do not keep them on the disk that will be in the drive during a session.)

When files are being transmitted either way, Communicate displays its progress at the bottom of the screen, telling you how much has been transferred, how long it expects to take to finish the job and how many errors it has spotted and corrected. At the end, the main screen will show whether the transfer has been completed successfully or not. There are a number of possible reasons for failure – the other user may not be available, the wanted file may not be there, there may not be enough disk space free, or the telephone line may be generating too many errors.

With the **single** option, you will only need to give the name of the file to be sent or received. Note that this must be the *full* file name, including the three-letter extension. So, a Write file called 'MAYMEMO' would be identified as 'MAYMEMO.XTX'; Spreadsheets have a '.XSS' extension; Database files have '.XDB', and Graphs '.XGR'.

The on-line commands

The **many** option needs a little preparatory work. Before you start the Communicate session, create a list of the filenames with Write. Then give the name of that Write file after you select the many option. The regional manager who has put together an illustrated report on the last quarter's business, and is about to send it to the central office, might create this Write file.

        SPRING.XTX
        SPRING.XSS
        SPRING.XGR
        SPR-MEMO.XTX

If the Write file was called 'SPR_SET', then that would be the name given within the **many** routine.

Closing Down

You should use **modem – hangup** to end a call, and must do so if you want to remain inside Communicate so that the system can be left in **answer** mode. But if you are closing down completely, or returning to the Library screen to select a new Communicate file, then just press **[F10]**. The system will hang up the telephone for you as it closes down.

■ SECTION 48
Keyboard macros

After you have been using Ability for a while, you will realise that there are some things that you type regularly. These may be command sequences, or chunks of text such as letter headings. You can cut down on typing time by writing macros into the function keys, so that a single press on a status key and an [F] key will produce the whole sequence.

```
                        Keyboard Macros

          Press Shift and                      Press Ctrl and
F1 [Mercurian Pulp Products/F2]    F1 [/F2OPP40/ENTLO/ENTR70/ENT/ESC]
F2 [F2F+TODAY()/ENT/F4FDL/ESC/]    F2 [                              ]
F3 [                          ]    F3 [                              ]
F4 [                          ]    F4 [                              ]
F5 [/CH/F7/CE/ENT/F5          ]    F5 [                              ]
F6 [                          ]    F6 [                              ]
F7 [/CH/F7/CE/F2BY            ]    F7 [                              ]
F8 [                          ]    F8 [                              ]
F9 [                          ]    F9 [                              ]
F10[/F2OFS/ENT                ]    F10[                              ]
          Press Alt and                        Press Alt and
F1 [                          ]    F6 [                              ]
F2 [                          ]    F7 [                              ]
F3 [                          ]    F8 [                              ]
F4 [                          ]    F9 [                              ]
F5 [                          ]    F10[                              ]
View or change keyboard macros
Enter :
F1 — Help
        F4 — Edit Field                        F10 — Done
```

FIGURE 48-1 The Macros screen

Macros are defined from the Library screen. Call up the commands and select **other**, then **macros**. The macros screen (Figure 48.1) has three sets on it – one for each of the status keys, [Shift], [Ctrl] and [Alt], and ten fields within each. Each combination of status and [F] key can be defined to hold a different macro, though in practice few people would want to use more than half a dozen or so. If you have too many, it could take as long to look up the purpose of each as it would to type the sequence that the macro replaces.

■ SECTION 48
Keyboard macros

A macro can include *any* keystrokes, not just letter and number keys but also functions and those that control cursor movement. These special keystrokes have to be written using the codes shown in Figure 48.2. They are easy enough to remember as they are essentially a slash followed by the initial or abbreviation.

Keystroke	Code	Keystroke	Code	Keystroke	Code
F1	/F1	Left	/L	Ctrl Left	/CL
F2	/F2	Right	/R	Ctrl Right	/CR
F3	/F3	Up	/U	Ctrl Up	/CU
F4	/F4	Down	/D	Ctrl Down	/CD
F5	/F5	Home	/H	Ctrl Home	/CH
F6	/F6	End	/END	Ctrl End	/CE
F7	/F7	Pg Up	/PU	Enter	/ENT
F8	/F8	Pg Dn	/PD	Escape	/ESC
F9	/F9	Ins	/I	Tab	/T
F10	/F10	.Del	/X	Shift Tab	/BT

FIGURE 48-2 Keystrokes

Type the macro sequences into the chosen key combinations, using **[F4]** to edit if necessary, then press **[F10]** when you have done. The macros will be stored on disk with the other system information and will be there whenever you use Ability in the future.

Sample macros – Save and Carry on

The first stage in creating a new macro takes place not on the macros screen, but in Write, the Spreadsheet or wherever the keystroke sequence is to be used. Run through the sequence as normal, taking careful note of which keys are pressed. What are the *exact* keystrokes in a command sequence? What function or cursor keys do you press? When do you press **[Enter]**?

A useful and simple macro to define is one that allows you to save the current file without closing down and returning to the Library screen. The sequence is the same, whether in Write, Graph or the Spreadsheet:

Keystroke	Macro characters	Effect
[F2]	/F2	Call up Commands
[O]	O	select Other
[F]	F	select File
[S]	S	select Save
[Enter]	/ENT	use the current filename

■ SECTION 48
Keyboard macros

The macro could be defined into [Shift] – **[F10]** by moving the screen cursor to that slot then typing:

/F2OFS/ENT

Thereafter, press **[F10]**, as normal, to save and exit, or **[shift]** – **[F10]** to save and carry on.

Letter Heading

If you start your letters with the name and address centred at the top of the page, you will actually type something like this:

```
Mercurian Pulp Products    [F2] Centre  [Enter]
Lennox House               [F2] Centre  [Enter]
...etc
```

This can be written into a macro – the limit is 250 characters, which should be more than enough.

Mercurian Pulp Product/F2C/ENTLennox House/F2C/Ent.....

Where the letter heading is to appear on the right of the page, write a set of [tab] and [right] keystrokes in before the text – observe how many of each you would use if typing the heading in directly:

/T/T/T/T/T/T/R/R/RMercurian Pulp Product/ENT/T/T/T/T/ T/T/R/R/RLen..

Today's Date

This is something which is regularly needed, and takes a little while to type as you have to set the date format and the field width. Working from within Spreadsheet, the sequence would be:

Keystroke	Macro characters	Effect
+TODAY()	+TODAY()	Today function
[Enter]	/ENT	enter into field
[F4]	/F4	call up Edit Field
[F]	F	select Format
[D]	D	select Date
[L]	L	Long, e.g. January 20,1988
[Esc]	/ESC	back to Date sub-menu
[Esc]	/ESC	exit back to spreadsheet
[F4]	/F4	– Edit Field again
[W]	W	select Width
[S] 20	S20	Set the width to 20 characters
[Esc]	/ESC	exit back to spreadsheet

This translates to the macro:

+TODAY()/ENT/F4FDL/ESC/ESC/F4WS20/ESC

Keyboard macros

If the macro was to be used within Write, you would need to slot two extra keystrokes in at the beginning to define a field, and the width-setting would be unnecessary. The macro becomes:

/F2F+TODAY()/ENT/F4FDL/ESC/ESC

Write the Spreadsheet version into [shift] – **[F1]** and the Write version into [Ctrl] – **[F1]**.

Page Formatting

If you have a standard format for your letters, and it is different from the default page layout, why not write it into a macro. Then a single operation will replace the page-length and left and right margin setting commands.

/F2OPP50/ENTL5/ENTR70/ENT/ESC

This gives the sequence:

[**F2**] **O**thers **P**age-format **P**age-length **50** [**Ent**er] **L**eft-margin **5** [**Ent**er] **R**ight-margin **70** [**Ent**er] [**Esc**ape]

■ SECTION 49
Making a Presentation

Some people will see **Presentation!** as the icing on Ability's cake; others will view it as froth on the beer. Could you make use of this computerised slide-show? It only takes half an hour or so to put a presentation together, so why not give it a try and see for yourself?

Start by taking 'snapshots' of the screen within Ability, to capture those graphs, tables and documents that you want to include in your show. Then switch to the Presentation! software to edit and link those screens together. The final result is a timed sequence of screen shots, which might be used as part of a presentation at a sales conference, or for a short demo at an exhibition or in a shop.

Taking Snapshots

Ability redefines the big [+] key (to the right of the numberpad) as a camera button. Whenever you press this, it will attempt to store the working screen – the top 21 lines – on disk in a snapshot library. This can be set up from the Library screen by using the **snapshot** command – which simply asks for a name for the library file. If you have not set up a library, then it can be done when you try to take the first snapshot. Type in the file name at the prompt:

Name of snapshot library: SALESNAP

If you pressed [+] by mistake – and it is easily done if you have been in the habit of using that key for its proper purpose – then press **[Esc]** to abort the snapshot.

Disk Usage

Note that each snapshot will take just over 16k of disk space. This can create problems, especially if you are working with floppy disks. If the data disk has already got a lot of files on it, there may not be enough room for all the snapshots that you want to take.

Wherever you store the snapshots initially, they must be on the Presentation! disk before you can edit and link them. As you can group several snapshot files into a single presentation, one solution to the lack of disk space would be to take the shots a few at a time.

Find out how much free space there is on the data disk, before you start. Take as many snapshots as will fit, then stop. Go back to DOS and copy the library file onto the Presentation! disk. Erase those snapshots from the data disk, and start again on the next set.

■ SECTION 49
Making a Presentation

Presentation!

The Presentation! software is not an integral part of the Ability system, although you can run it from the Library screen if the disk is in the Active drive. Point to **present** in the Other Programs list and press **[Enter]**. You will be prompted:

Remainder of command line:

Ignore this and just press **[Enter]** again.

It may be easier to run it from DOS. To do this, slot the Presentation! disk into drive A: and type '**present**'. Either way, you will reach the title and then the working screen. Give the name of the snapshot library, or of the file containing the first set of snapshots, and you are ready to start putting the presentation together.

All that is really essential is to set the style of **transition** from screen to screen, and the **timing** of each display. You can also alter the display sequence, add text and symbols to the screens, and delete unwanted screens or pull in more from another library file. It is also possible to arrange for a snatch of 'music' to be played as each screen appears, but this is best kept for audiences that are tone deaf or in need of some comic relief.

```
            PRESENTATION! — display creation

 DISPLAY
 SEQUENCE        TITLE            TRANSITION     TUNE    TIMING
     1           SCR1
     2           SCR2
     3           SCR3
     4           SCR4
     5           SCR5
                 << NEW >>



Presentation: SALESNAP.SNA                    85% Free

F1 — Help
F2 — Commands                                  F10 —Done
```

FIGURE 49-1 Presentation working screen

■ SECTION 49
Making a Presentation

Browsing and Re-Titling

The first job will probably be to give the screens more meaningful titles to replace the initial 'SCR1', 'SCR2', 'SCR3', labels. If you cannot remember what each contained, look through the screens, using the **browse** command. Move the cursor to the title field (or any other along the same line), press **[F2]** and select browse. The screen will be displayed.

To give a new title, just move the cursor onto the title and type its new name.

Re-ordering

By default, the display sequence will be the order in which the snapshots were taken. To move a snapshot to a new position, retype its number so that it shows the screen which it is to follow. So, if you want screen 1 to follow screen 2, re-number it as **2A**. Where you want to slot several screens in together, use other letters – 2B, 2C, 2D. It can be a bit of a messy process, but when you have finished renumbering, use the **re-order** command, and this will tidy things up again. Figure 49.2 illustrates this. Here the first and fourth screen are to be fitted in after the second.

```
OLD SEQUENCE       RE-NUMBERING         AFTER RE-ORDER

1    SCR1          2A   SCR1            1    SCR2
2    SCR2          2    SCR2            2    SCR1
3    SCR3          3    SCR3            3    SCR4
4    SCR4          2B   SCR4            4    SCR3
```

FIGURE 49-2 Re-ordering snapshots

Transitions

You must set the style of transition from one screen to the next. Position the cursor on the TRANSITION field, call up the commands and select **transition**. You will be offered a choice of eight styles:

```
LR   —   Left to Right scroll
RL   —   Right to Left scroll
TB   —   Top to Bottom scroll
BT   —   Bottom to Top scroll
SQ   —   Shrinking Square, the screen vanishing into the middle
V4   —   Vertical blinds, 4 slices scrolling simultaneously
H4   —   Horizontal blinds
D4   —   Diagonal blinds, 4 slices in each corner of the screen
```

Making a Presentation

The shrinking square and the simpler blinds all give good crisp transitions between screens.

Timing

This must be set if the sequence is to run through automatically. If you leave the timing column blank, then when you **view** the presentation, you will get this prompt after each screen:

Press [F10] to EXIT, [↑] to go back 1 screen, or [↓] to continue.

This can be useful when you are still working on the design. It could also be a good way to run a presentation if you are not sure how long you want to keep each screen in view.

To set the timing, just type in the number of seconds that you want to hold the screen after its music, if any, has been played.

Viewing the Presentation

Once the basic sequence has been set, you can view the presentation at any time. Move the cursor to the first screen's row – if you want to start from the beginning – then press **[F2]** and select **view**.

Tunes

I'm sure these are not to be taken seriously. After all, anyone who can take eight badly timed and off-key beeps and call it Beethoven's *Fifth Symphony*, has got to be joking. Some of the jingles are quite jolly, and might serve to attract people's attention, but will it get them into the right frame of mind for receiving the message your presentation is trying to get across? Try a few and see what you think.

Position the cursor in the tune column, press **[F2]** and select **music**. Choose then from the sub-menu:

Happy Sad Familiar Other

Which brings you to these alternatives:

Happy – Hornpipe, Three Cheers, Sparkle, Wake up, Fanfare, Long Fanfare, Up slide.
Wake Up and the Up slide are not too bad. One-beeper fanfares are non-starters, and the Hornpipe is so fast it would tie a sailor's legs in knots.

■ SECTION 49
Making a Presentation

Sad –   Beethoven's *Fifth*, Down slide, Curtains.
Curtains is the start of the *Funeral March* and is awful, so is the *Fifth*. The Down slide is unobjectionable.

Familiar – Shave & a Haircut, Pomp & Circumstance, Blue Yonder, Bell Tones, French National Anthem, Circus Music, Wedding March.
The Bell Tones are beepy, but acceptable; the Circus is very jolly as is Shave & a Haircut. The rest are forgettable.

Other –   Sousa March, Pop goes the Weasel, Happy Birthday, Jolly Good Fellow, Jingle Bells, William Tell Overture, 1812 Overture, Hail to the Chief.
Happy Birthday and Jolly Good Fellow are OK. Reagan would need to be on horseback to keep up with this Hail to the Chief, and the classics are mangled as usual.

Remember that the delay set by the timing only starts after the tune has finished. As the tunes are of variable length, you will have to play this by ear.

Adding Text and Symbols

You cannot edit the text that was on the screen when the snapshot was taken, but you can add new text and brighten up the appearance with a selection of symbols.

With the cursor on the title of the screen to be decorated, press **[F2]** and select **add**. From the sub-menu, choose between **text** or **symbols**.

Text may be any size from normal to seven times normal, and may be slanted over to the right to varying extents. (The maximum slant of 3 is about 30 degrees.) For extra emphasis, the letters can be shadowed, as in Figure 49.3.

 Bright New Ideas

FIGURE 49-3 Presentation text and symbols

The **symbols** range from arrows and lines through to little pictures of bells, medicine bottles, a sad face (!), even a birthday cake. These are probably more suitable for an office party than a serious business conference, and rather like the tunes they raise the question of what kind of message you are trying to put over with your presentation.

After you have defined your text or selected a symbol, the screen will display the snapshot with the additional material super-imposed on the top left. This can be manoeuvred into place with the cursor keys – and you will see that it slides over, but does not obliterate, the underlying screen. When you are satisfied with the position, press **[F10]** to fix it. And if you decide that it was the wrong typeface, or the wrong symbol, press **[Esc]** instead to abandon it.

■ SECTION 49
Making a Presentation

Writing on a Blank Screen

You may want a title page for your presentation, or information pages between the snapshots. This is where the << **NEW** >> screen comes in. At the bottom of the display list, there will always be << NEW >>. Put your cursor on that and give it a title, then use **add** to write your title, slogan, memo or whatever.

Adding and Deleting Snapshots

If you want to cut a screen out of the presentation, but would like to leave it in that library for later use, type an '**X**' next to its display number – '4X' or whatever.

To remove a snapshot from a library permanently, move the cursor onto its title and use the **delete** command. A snapshot cannot be recovered once deleted.

To bring additional snapshots into the presentation, use the **file** command to **load** in another library. The snapshots will be added to the end of the current list, and can then be linked into the existing sequence.

Save and Group-save

These **file** options will allow you to save an individual snapshot, or a set of them, in a new file. They may then be incorporated into a different presentation with **load**.

To **save** a single snapshot, point the cursor to its title before calling up the command.

Group-saves are a little more complicated. You must first reorder the display list, so that the snapshots to be saved are all together at the bottom. Then point the cursor to the topmost title and call up **file group-save**.

Starting on a New Library

If you want to set up a second presentation in the same working session, use the **library** command to load in the new library file. The current presentation will be saved, complete with any alterations that you have made, before the new file is loaded in.

■ SECTION 49
Making a Presentation

Running the Presentation

While you are inside the Presentation! program, the current sequence can always be run by selecting the **view** command. If all you want to do is to run a prepared presentation, then it is quicker and almost as simple to run it from DOS.

Insert the Presentation! disk, complete with the relevant library file, into the active drive. At the prompt type:

A> **present view salesnap**

This will start up Presentation!. Select the view command and load in the file – here called 'salesnap'. It will then run through its sequence, and at the end return to DOS.

■ SECTION 50
Ability Plus

Ability Plus may cost twice as much as Ability, but do not expect twice as many features. These things do not work that way. After all, a Montego may cost twice as much as a Mini, but it still only has four wheels. The higher price reflects the presence of several substantial additions to the package and a scatter of small, but significant, improvements to Write, Spreadsheet and Database.

Perhaps the most obvious extra feature is that Ability Plus has a spelling checker that can be called up from within either Write or Database. With a basic dictionary of nearly 150,000 words and the facility to allow you to build up your own specialised addenda, the checker should be able to cope with anything that you can throw at it. A spelling checker is a useful tool, and it is not just for poor spellers! We all make typing errors and it is very easy to miss them when you are writing in a hurry. A quick skim through with the spelling checker at the end, and those odd errors will be spotted for you. It is far quicker than proof-reading, and much more accurate. The only failure of a checker is that it will not pick up those words that were mis-typed but still make real words – 'their' instead of 'there', 'of' for 'off', 'commuter' not 'computer'.

The second big plus is that you can split the screen into two windows, within Write and the Spreadsheet. The split can be vertical or horizontal, and each window can be controlled independently. This allows you to bring two distant parts of a large spreadsheet onto the same screen, so that as data is entered into one part, its effect on the results can be seen in the other. In a Write file, a window split will let you refer back to earlier text without breaking off from your writing.

If a file is in use in the other flip state, then it will be automatically pulled into the second window. This makes it far easier to read and to pick up data from one file to put down in the other. The normal flip facility works well enough where you only want to move a single block of data, but is cumbersome to use if you need to refer constantly to the other file.

■ SECTION 50
Ability Plus

New import/export facilities have extended Ability's compatibility with other software. The routines will convert files produced by such major packages as Lotus 1-2-3, dBASE and Multimate, into a form that Ability can read. Another valuable, if somewhat unfriendly, addition is the drivers program that will enable you to produce your own printer and plotter drivers – those programs that convert printing and typestyle settings into codes for the printer. Ability Plus can therefore be used with *any* printer or plotter.

The last of the substantial additions is the Lotus-style macro command language. Ability's macros are useful conveniences that let you compress a sequence of key-strokes into a two-key combination. The Plus macros allow you to automate a whole set of operations, so that, for example, a non-specialist user could update a spreadsheet. You can prompt your user for an input and collect the data into a chosen field; perform any of the normal commands; write password protection into a file; you can even set up new line menus on screen and perform a different set of commands depending upon the selection from that menu.

The other improvements in Plus may be less striking, but they can make the difference between a good level of presentation and a professional level. In Write, there are subscripts and superscripts so that mathematical formulae can be written, or 'small print' included in your documents. The lines can be set at single, double or triple spacing, and you can end a page wherever you like, rather than being forced to remain within fixed page sizes. The addition of a **block-save** command makes it easier to extract a chunk of text and store it in a new file – something which would require a pick up, flip and put down sequence in Ability.

In Plus's Database, you can specify the type of data that must be entered into a field on a form. This is a small alteration, but it can substantially reduce errors in data entry. The Spreadsheet allows you to scale the X-axis of a graph, as well as the Y-axis – you may not want the facility very often, but it is nice to know that it is there. In both Spreadsheet and Write, you can set field formats throughout the file with the new global format command – handy where the bulk of fields are all to handle numbers in the same way.

204

■ SECTION 50
Ability Plus

Communicate has been extended to include the excellent XMODEM file transfer routines, though Presentation! is unchanged – those of us waiting for decent music in Presentation! will have to keep on waiting.

Ability Plus is totally compatible with Ability, so that the files that you have created can be reused without any alteration. There are some variations in the command menus which take a bit of getting used to, but are worth it. They have regrouped commands in those long menus – the ones that ended with **other** – so that the most frequently used commands are easier to find.

So, is it worth upgrading to Ability Plus? The trade-in arrangement means that an Ability owner can get Plus for just over £100, so it is not expensive. If you are using Ability regularly, then the improved efficiency and presentation could soon justify the outlay. Ability is a good package. Ability Plus is better.

Index

Index